Overcoming the

FIVE OBSTACLES
TO ASSURANCE

Your Winning Game Plan for Making
Your Calling and Election Sure!

FRANK T. WHALEN

ISBN 979-8-89112-159-1 (Paperback)
ISBN 979-8-89112-161-4 (Hardcover)
ISBN 979-8-89112-160-7 (Digital)

Copyright © 2024 Frank T. Whalen
All rights reserved
First Edition

All Bible verses cited are from the English Standard Version unless otherwise noted.

All rights reserved. No part of this publication may be reproduced, distributed, or transmitted in any form or by any means, including photocopying, recording, or other electronic or mechanical methods without the prior written permission of the publisher. For permission requests, solicit the publisher via the address below.

Covenant Books
11661 Hwy 707
Murrells Inlet, SC 29576
www.covenantbooks.com

CONTENTS

ACKNOWLEDGMENTS

There are four individuals I would like to acknowledge and thank for their profound influence on me and the completion of this book.

First, to my dad, Francis M. Whalen, who instilled in me a great love and respect for the Bible from an early age.

To the late Don Sullivan, my football coach in college, who showed me the true way of salvation.

To Dr. David Brewer, who has been my Barnabas, encouraging me to press on until I finish this work.

Finally, and most importantly, to the omnipotent Son of God and Captain of the Host of Heaven, Jesus Christ of Nazareth, my Lord and my Savior.

1

GAME PLAN—PHASE 1: BIG PICTURE

ESTABLISHING THE CONTEXT FOR ASSURANCE

I began to find my soul to be assaulted with fresh doubts...
How can you tell you are elected? And what if you should
not? By these things I was driven to my wits' end.[1]
—John Bunyan

Sinclair Ferguson defines *assurance* of salvation as "the confidence that we have been justified and accepted by God in Christ, regenerated by his Spirit, and adopted into his family, and that through faith in him we will be kept for the day when our justification and adoption are consummated in the regeneration of all things."[2]

In my research of the topic of assurance, I have come across no better definition than Ferguson provides. However, for many people the "confidence" Ferguson refers to waxes and wanes. For some individuals, the lack of assurance causes extreme psychological and

---

[1] John Bunyan, Grace Abounding to the Chief of Sinners (London, The Religious Tract Society, 1905), 29.
[2] Sinclair Ferguson, The Reformation and Assurance (The Banner of Truth, no. 643, April 2017), 20.

emotional crisis, and despite their struggles in pursuit of confident assurance, it remains elusive.

Millions of Christians throughout the ages have dealt with this difficult problem with little understanding of its cause or remedy. The primary goal of this book is to provide a thorough understanding of the root causes of assurance-doubt, and how to gain victory over it.

The subtitle of this book is *Your Winning Game Plan for Making Your Calling and Election Sure!* I played and coached football for many years and received and developed hundreds of game plans for the opponents we faced. In thinking about how to effectively organize my research, and an overarching theme to tie it all together, I decided to stick with what I knew!

If you are a member of the fairer sex, or are not a fan of football, don't worry—this book is still for you. The only prerequisite you need to get everything out of the information I will share is a desire to gain the assurance of your salvation or help someone do the same.

That said, a game plan is simply a set of strategies and tactics to help you solve specific challenges presented by the opposition. Game plans include actionable steps to implement, achieve, and evaluate the goals you set.

The process of developing a football game plan is systematic and meticulous. It requires a lot of time and is very hard work. Coaches put in seemingly endless hours watching game film, analyzing data, and conducting meetings, let alone the time spent on the field implementing and perfecting the game plan in practice.

Don't worry, we won't watch any film or attend any staff meetings as part of our game plan. However, we will utilize the same thorough and logical approach football coaches employ. We will diligently search the Scriptures and glean insights from leading experts in the fields of theology, medicine, and psychology. No stone will be left unturned in the development of our game plan for achieving a lasting assurance of salvation.

To develop a sound game plan, coaches begin by gathering as much general information regarding the opponent as possible. We first look at our history with the opponent. How familiar are we with them? Are they a conference rival? Is this a team that we have traditionally struggled against? After considering our history with the opponent, we turn our attention to current circumstances. What is their win-loss record? Where are they in the conference rankings? Any historical or recent data on our opponent is considered important and noted.

As coaches, we also need to set the game itself in proper perspective. We explain to our players how the outcome of the game affects our team's trajectory for the rest of the season. Players are also made aware of the impact the game has on their individual goals. In short, we build a case on why this game is important.

The venue is also a factor to be considered. Is it a home game or away? How much of a home field advantage will the visiting team have to overcome? As an aside, this is a very important consideration in our assurance game plan. Although I won't develop it now, I dedicate an entire chapter (chapter 4, "The Venue") to this subject.

Game plans are developed and organized in phases, and a "big-to-small" approach always works best. Before any film is watched on our opponents, or analysis is done on their schemes and tendencies, this baseline information on the opposing team and the implications of the game must be gathered. Setting our opponent and the game itself in proper context is the first phase of a successful game plan that cannot be skipped.

Thus, as you progress through this book it's best to read each chapter in order. Don't skip ahead or jump around, as each chapter is built upon the foundation of the previous ones. Take your time and read the information meditatively. Remember, the subtitle of this book is *Your Winning Game Plan for Making Your Calling and Election Sure!*, with the emphasis on, *"Your."* To that end, there will be one or two questions/assignments at the end of each chapter to help you think more deeply about the material presented. Most importantly, ask the Holy Spirit to reveal the specifics of your own struggles with assurance, and for the strength and grace to overcome them.

So think of this opening chapter as the first phase of our game plan, where we set the problem of assurance of salvation in proper context. Phase 1 of our game plan will consist of four separate sections and is foundational to the rest of the information presented in this book.

In the first of these four sections, I will briefly state how my own struggles with assurance began. Indeed, I write this book with a long and often painful history with this issue. However, I am by no means alone in this struggle, so the second section will focus on the pervasiveness of this problem, currently and in past generations. The final two sections of phase 1 of our game plan will focus on the magnitude of the issue itself. We will look at biblical passages regarding the importance of assurance, as well as the impact assurance-doubt has on an individual and the church as a whole.

1. *Personal history with the problem*

I mentioned that football coaches begin game planning by examining their history and familiarity with their opponent. Understanding how, when, and most importantly, why our struggles with assurance first began is also extremely important for our game plan for assurance. Though this is not an autobiography, with the intent of making the information presented understandable and relevant; I will occasionally interject the circumstances of my own struggles with assurance which first began many years ago in college. In fact, much of the information I share corresponds precisely to the major trials and tribulations in my walk as a Christian and how God used those experiences to strengthen and settle me in my assurance.

As Peter promised in his first epistle, I am confident that the information provided in this book will be one of the means that God uses to grant you the full and lasting assurance that has been absent in your life.

> But the God of all grace, who hath called us unto his eternal glory by Christ Jesus, after that ye have suffered a while, make you perfect, stablish, strengthen, settle you. (1 Peter 5:10 KJV)

What follows is how my struggle with the assurance of salvation began. I was born and raised as a Roman Catholic but ended up going to a Presbyterian college mainly because of its proximity to home and to play football. Many of my teammates were also Catholic and chose the college for the same reason.

The strict code of conduct at the college was viewed by many of us Catholics as a negative to tolerate, like the un-air-conditioned dorm rooms or subpar cafeteria food! We were constantly causing the college grief with our drinking, cussing, and overall nasty behavior. I certainly was a notorious offender! To be clear, I am not blaming our behavior on Roman Catholicism; I only mention it to put the following account in perspective.

During an evening study session, one of the professors got exasperated with our incessant misconduct. She suddenly stopped the review, and stated, "You Catholics think you can act like the devil all week, confess your sins to a priest, and all will be fine. However, there is one sin you will never be forgiven of, and that is blasphemy against the Holy Spirit!"

Though her theology and exegesis of this sin was suspect, the first part of her statement described me exactly! I truly thought that if I went to Mass, performed the sacraments, and did my penance, then I'd be fine. No matter what my behavior was like, God would always forgive me. Her spot-on description of my behavior and thoughts gave her warning against blasphemy of the Spirit much more authority in my estimation.

Even though I never heard of, "blasphemy of the Holy Spirit," the prospects of never being forgiven and spending an eternity in hell filled me with extreme anxiety. Despite having no idea what blasphemy of the Holy Spirit was, my mind fixated on it. I assumed blasphemy was swearing, and so I tried to block cuss words directed towards the Holy Spirit from entering my mind. John Bunyan, the author of *Pilgrim's Progress*, recounts the same dreadful experience in his autobiography, *Grace Abounding to the Chief of Sinners*.

> In these days, when I have heard others talk
> of what was the sin against the Holy Ghost, then

would the tempter so provoke me to desire to sin that sin, that I was as if I could not, must not, neither should be quiet until I had committed it; now no sin would serve but that. If it were to be committed by speaking of such a word, then I have been as if my mouth would have spoken that word, whether I would or no; and in so strong a measure was this temptation upon me, that often I have been ready to clap my hand under my chin, to hold my mouth from opening; and to that end also, I have had thoughts at other times, to leap with my head downward, into some muckhill-hole or other, to keep my mouth from speaking.[3]

I now know, and will discuss this phenomenon later, that attempts to stop thinking certain thoughts has the opposite effect, and not surprisingly my thoughts became a waking nightmare lasting for months.

It did not occur to me at the time why my mind would fixate on this, when the professor's words seemed to have no effect on my fellow classmates. In addition, I did not grasp that my constant fighting of this thought proved my repulsion of it, and not my desire to commit it. These revelations would also come later for me, and their psychological and neuro-medical explanations will be addressed in subsequent chapters of this book.

Nonetheless, this miserable ordeal had a profound impact on me. Even after I became a Christian a couple of years later, and knew my misunderstandings regarding blasphemy of the Spirit, I still periodically struggled with doubts concerning the assurance of my salvation. The explanations for these seemingly unexpected seasons of doubt will also be developed further as we walk through the *five obstacles to the assurance of salvation.*

---

[3] John Bunyan, *Grace Abounding.*

At this point, some of you may not be able to pinpoint exactly when, how, or why your struggles with assurance began. That's okay; as you read through this book, you will begin to understand the causative reasons. For now, however its best to continue to set this topic in its proper context. The following sections will shed light on how pervasive struggles with assurance are and why the Bible places such a high priority for the resolution of this age-old problem.

2. *Prevalence of the problem*

Along with considering their team's history with the opponent, I mentioned that coaches also make note of their opponent's reputation and current status. To put the problem of assurance in proper perspective we must do the same.

Struggles with the assurance of salvation is by no means a new phenomenon. The issue cannot be attributed to our modern frenetic lifestyle. Our culture's emphasis on feeling as opposed to reason is not the singular cause, nor are such doubts a sole consequence of our lack of biblical knowledge.

Many giants of the faith have dealt with seasons of great anxiety regarding the reality of their salvation. The opening quote listed is from *Grace Abounding to the Chief of Sinners*, the autobiography of John Bunyan. In *Grace Abounding*, Bunyan records the turmoil produced by incessant doubts concerning his salvation, and specifics of Bunyan's struggles will be examined later in this book. Suffice to say, many heroes of the faith, from King David to Charles Spurgeon, all wrestled at times with this issue.

Charles Haddon Spurgeon, the great "prince of preachers," routinely filled the six-thousand-seat auditorium of London's Metropolitan Tabernacle to the rafters with his powerfully captivating sermons. Nevertheless, Spurgeon struggled at times with depression, which often manifested in excruciating doubts regarding the reality of his own salvation. One season of his despondency was so painful that he affirmed, "I could say with Job, 'My soul chooseth strangling rather than life [Job 7:15]. I could readily enough have laid violent hands upon myself, to escape from my misery of spirit."[4]

King David also had his own dark night of the soul, and a close look at David's struggles with assurance and how he eventually found victory will be addressed in chapter 8. However, struggles with assurance are not just reserved for individuals whom God uses to accomplish great advances in His kingdom. Countless un-renowned believers through the centuries have fought the same battle. Yet struggles with assurance are not confined to the saints of bygone generations, it remains a widespread concern.

In a recent poll, Barna[5] observes that although a majority of Americans believe in life after death (81 percent), and the existence of the soul (79 percent), few are clear about their ultimate destination. One in every four adults (24 percent,), representing a total of 50 million people, admitted that they are uncertain regarding their eternal fate. That is an astounding number of individuals!

Undoubtedly many of these people have developed various coping mechanisms to push that uncertainty, and the uncomfortable feelings associated with it, far from their conscious minds. However, for many people such psychological Band-Aids don't work anymore, or perhaps never did.

The Barna poll just referenced, revealed how pervasive the problem of assurance is for the entire country, but is assurance a problem for the Church as well? Writing in the Journal of the American Society for Church Growth, Dr. Henry Schmidt analyzed the data of a weeklong religious crusade held in California. His data showed that 11 percent of attendees confirmed that their compelling need was to gain assurance of their salvation.[6]

---

4   C. H. Spurgeon, *Metropolitan Tabernacle Pulpit Sermons* (London: Passmore & Alabaster, 1855–1917), vol. 36, 200.

5   George Barna, *Americans Describe Their Views about Life after Death* (The Barna Group, Ltd., 2009).

6   H. J. Schmidt, "Crusade Decisions: Counting and Accounting for Lost Sheep" (Journal of the American Society for Church Growth, 1 no. (1), 1990): 16–40, retrieved from https://digitalarchives.apu.edu/jascg/ vol1/iss1/3.

Although the church has moved from conducting such large-scale outreach methods in lieu of small group discipleship programs; the data collected from these big events is revealing. If one extrapolates the data from Schmidt's findings across the major cities of this country, the number of Christians desperately seeking assurance is alarming.

As mentioned earlier, lack of assurance is not simply a matter that can be chalked up to biblical ignorance. R. C. Sproul recounts a survey taken while he was in seminary in which 90 percent of the graduating seniors said they were not sure of their salvation, and many even expressed anger at the question, seeing in it a kind of implied presumptuousness.[7] Though anecdotal, the survey provided by Sproul can be reproduced with similar results in seminaries throughout the world.

Finally, we have seen that the prevalence of assurance struggles is neither a minor, nor a modern problem. It is a pervasive and agonizing problem that respects no person, nor does it skip certain generations. Indeed, John dedicated an entire epistle to help a local community of believers with this exact concern.

> These things have I written unto you that believe on the name of the Son of God; that ye may know that ye have eternal life, and that ye may believe on the name of the Son of God. (1 John 5:13 KJV)

3. *Priority of pursuit*

As mentioned, the prevalence of this issue is not unique to certain eras, countries, denominations, or people. Moreover, the mental and emotional strain is experienced by all who struggle in this regard. Nevertheless, and in direct contrast to the objections of Sproul's

---

[7] R. C. Sproul, *The Holiness of God, Chosen by God, Pleasing God* (Peabody; Hendrickson Publishers, 1985), 246.

classmates, the Bible is clear as to the priority it places on believers to press on until full assurance is achieved.

Paul charges us to examine ourselves to see whether we are in the faith (2 Corinthians 13:5), and to work out our own salvation with fear and trembling (Philippians 2:12). Peter commands to confirm our calling and election (2 Peter 1:10).

Martin Luther, the great Reformer, whose own struggles with assurance are well chronicled, offers the same direction; "But we must be assured and out of doubt that we are under grace, that we please God for Christ's sake, and that we have the Holy Ghost."[8] Exegeting 1 John 5:13, John Calvin also affirms the importance of pursuing assurance:

> As there ought to be a daily progress in faith,
> so he [i.e., John] says he wrote to those who had
> already believed, so that they might believe more
> firmly and with greater certainty, and thus enjoy
> a fuller confidence as to eternal life.[9]

Finally, the Westminster Divines also placed a high degree of importance upon this subject, dedicating to it an entire chapter in the Westminster Confession of Faith. For those unfamiliar with the WCF, it is a thorough and brilliant document composed at the behest of the English Parliament in the seventeenth century. Its purpose was to provide clarity regarding issues of doctrine, worship, and a wide range of other topics for the Church of England. Over a hundred pastors and scholars (divines) were called upon to compose it. Since its completion the WCF has been adopted by thousands of churches across many denominational lines and is still in use today.

In chapter 18 of the WCF, "Of Assurance of Grace and Salvation," sections 1 and 2, the divines make three separate observations. First, that assurance is possible, *"There is a true assurance amounting to an*

---

[8] Martin Luther, *A Commentary on Saint Paul's Epistle to the Galatians* (London; B. Blake, November 14, 2009), 296.

[9] John Calvin, *Commentaries on the Catholic Epistles* (Princeton; Princeton Theological Seminary Library, February; 2009), digitized 264.

infallible certainty." Second, the divines echo Luther and Calvin in affirming that assurance must be pursued, *"And therefore it is the duty of everyone to give all diligence to make his calling and election sure."* Lastly, that assurance is separate from faith, *"This infallible assurance doth not so belong to the essence of faith, but that a true believer may wait long, and conflict with many difficulties, before he be partaker of it."* This third statement is especially important to the main thrust of this book as it portends the struggles associated with assurance-doubt.

It is also important to note that the WCF affirms that the doubts and difficulties experienced by believers as they pursue assurance are evidence for genuine faith and not its lack. Hodge provides additional insight in this regard.

> Assurance, in one degree or another of it, is of the essence of faith, because just in proportion to the strength of our faith is our assurance of the truth of that which we believe; but since true faith exists in various degrees of strength, and since its exercises are sometimes intermitted, it follows that the assurance which accompanies true faith is not always a full assurance.[10]

The Bible and great theologians of church history place immense priority on the subject of assurance not just because of the widespread prevalence of concern among God's people, but also because of the inherent importance of the issue itself.

I mentioned that creating a sense of urgency in football players early in the game planning process was critical to focus their attention on the importance of the task before them. We must have that same type of focus and urgency regarding the importance of assurance to overcome its major obstacles. The best way to create that type of motivation is to consider the stakes that are involved. With that in mind, let's look at the last section of phase 1 in our game plan.

---

[10] A. A. Hodge, *The Westminster Confession of Faith: A Commentary* (Carlisle, PA; The Banner of Truth Trust, 2002), 244.

4. *Primacy of possessing*

Coaches create "buy-in" from their player's by explaining why the upcoming game is critical for achieving personal and team goals. To obtain the same level of urgency and commitment to achieve the goal of assurance, we also must know what's at stake, for us personally, and for the church.

So why is assurance so critical for the believer? What are the consequences of living out your life as a Christian with little or fleeting assurance? More importantly, how does our level of assurance affect our understanding of God?

This may seem odd, but to help answer these questions we will look at an insightful old Japanese folktale. This ancient story is called "Tsuru no Ongaeshi"; it literally means "Crane Returns a Favor." When told today, it is often titled simply as, "The Crane Wife." There are several versions of this legend, and with your indulgence, I will share my favorite.

As the story goes, there was once a very poor young man named Karoku, who lived with his aged mother high in the mountains of Japan. Karoku made charcoal for a living and sold his wares to the people who lived in the village below. One winter, Karoku's mother sent him to the village with money to buy new bedding for the cold months ahead. On his way down the mountain, Karoku happened upon a crane who was caught in a trap. Karoku tried to free the crane, but the owner of the trap stopped him. Karoku offered to pay for the crane's release with the money he was given by his mother, and the man accepted Karoku's offer.

So Karoku freed the bird himself, and he watched it fly safely away before making his way back up the mountain. When he returned, he told his mother all that had happened. His mother agreed that Karoku did the right thing and assured him they would make do with their old bedding.

A few days later a beautiful woman knocked on Karoku's door. To Karoku's great surprise, the woman said that it was her desire to marry him! Karoku had never seen such a beautiful woman, but being honest as he was kind, he confessed that he was very poor and could not pay her dowry. The woman assured Karoku that no wedding gift was necessary. So the couple wed straightaway, and Karoku loved his wife with all his heart.

After several years, the couple fell on hard financial times. Karoku's wife told him that she would make an ornate cloth that he could sell to the ruler of the province. Her only stipulation was that Karoku must not watch her as she prepared this cloth. Karoku obeyed his wife's stipulations, and in three days, she emerged from the spare room of the house with a most exquisite fabric. Karoku took the cloth to the lord of the land who paid him a handsome price and offered even more money for a second cloth!

Karoku returned home and told his wife all that had transpired. His wife was so happy, and she agreed to make another cloth, but on the same condition that Karoku not watch her as she works. Once again, Karoku agreed to his wife's conditions. However, this time his wife was in the spare room working for many days, and Karoku became concerned. So quiet as a mouse, he opened the door to check on his wife. To his astonishment, he saw a crane that had all of its feathers plucked off and was weaving them into the cloth!

As Karoku stared in amazement, the crane spoke to him, "I am the crane you freed all those years ago, and I am also your wife. The cloth is finished. Please take it to the master of the land. However, now that you see me for who I really am I must go, because I am afraid that you won't love me anymore." Before Karoku could answer, a large flock of cranes came and helped her fly away.

Believers who lack assurance are in many ways like the crane-wife. They truly love the Lord and believe His Word. However, alongside that belief are doubts. Does God truly love and want me? Is God just waiting for me to screw up, so He can renege on His promise of salvation? How could God love me, seeing He knows everything about me? Questions such as these are constantly in their minds.

In response to such inaccurate assumptions concerning God's attitude and motivations, those who lack assurance may make "beautiful cloths" to win God's favor. They do this primarily by living an overly strict and ascetic lifestyle. However, even amid such appeasement efforts, they still try to stay hidden from His gaze. Such worries rob believers of their confidence and joy. As a result, fear, and distrust crawl in to fill the void. No relationship can flourish under such conditions. So like the crane-wife, people who lack assurance try to appease, hide, and distance themselves from their true love.

The similarities continue, as those who lack assurance may even return to their "old flock" for a season. Yet genuine believers never completely or permanently leave God, more importantly God never leaves them (Hebrews 13:5). However, some may gradually become content keeping God at arm's length and watching other believers from afar. Like a penniless person staring through a storefront window, they always feel like an outsider looking in.

Why is assurance important? Because without it we lack a sense of belonging. We have no confidence, joy, or trust. Without those three attributes, personal growth in the faith is stunted, and sustained diligence in Christian service is impossible. As D. L. Moody observed, "I never met anybody who ever did anything for the Lord who wasn't sure of his salvation."

Moreover, the belief that assurance can be lost forever along with one's salvation has a profound impact on a person's view of God and understanding of the totality of Scripture. Biblical grounds for eternal security will be addressed later, but it's appropriate now to affirm its importance. As to the weightiness of eternal security, Strombeck pulls no punches.

> The principal reason, however, for this volume is that unless one understands and accepts the doctrine of eternal security, one cannot accept without a great deal of reservation the doctrines of the grace of God. The whole body of grace truth loses very much of its meaning to those who reject the doctrine of eternal security.[11]

I mentioned that having the assurance of our salvation is not just critical for individual believers. Assurance is also crucial for the

---

[11] J. F. Strombeck, *Shall Never Perish* (Grand Rapids; Kregel Publications, 1991), 19.

proper function and health of the entire body of Christ. The church is a family made up of people, and when one member of the family struggles, we all do. Therefore, Jesus will seek for those who are struggling with assurance, not only for His great love for them personally, but for His entire church.

Christ, our great Shepherd, understands the importance of assurance, and is ever vigilant over the condition of His flock. Jesus is continuously molding and shaping us whether we are aware of it or not. He never grows tired of restoring His hurting sheep to full health, or lovingly correcting those who have gone wayward. Christ brings each of his lost ones back to the fold where they can use their gifts once again for the church, which is the perfect segue to finish telling the story of "The Crane-Wife."

Several years had passed since Karoku's wife had left. With the money he received for the two beautiful cloths, and some wise investments, Karoku was now a very rich man. Though he had amassed great wealth and had want of no material possessions, his heart still ached for his beloved wife. So Karoku set out, determined to search all of Japan to find her.

Despite his exhaustive search, Karoku could not find her. However, one day Karoku happened upon an old man who told him that he lived on an island called "the Robe of Crane Feathers." This name intrigued Karoku, so he asked the man to take him there. Once they arrived, the old man told Karoku where the large flock of cranes for which his island was named, could be found. Karoku took off running until he found the large pond where the cranes made their home.

In the middle of the pond, there was an island with hundreds of cranes huddled together, but Karoku could not see his wife among them. However, as Karoku waded towards the island the cranes began to separate, and there in the middle of the flock, stood a naked crane. Karoku had found her! As the crane locked eyes with Karoku, she stood before him regally, with her head held high. Karoku's diligent search dispelled all doubts from her heart of his undying love for her. She was no longer ashamed of her true appearance, in fact, she had now become the "queen of the cranes."

If you struggle with assurance, chances are elements of this old Japanese story resonate with you. You can see your own doubts and insecurities in Karoku's wife. You probably forgot how many times you have asked God to forgive and save you.

In attempts to gain assurance you may have fallen into legalism, heaping extrabiblical "dos and don'ts" upon yourself. However, no matter what you have tried, assurance never seems to stick. As a result, the pendulum may have swung the other way, with the telltale signs of distancing yourself from God and other believers. You don't pray nearly as much as you used to, seldom read your Bible, and attending church services has become spotty at best. Sound familiar? For some of you, it may have been years, decades even, since you have had a close fellowship with the Lord.

I know it may seem hopeless but remember there are two main characters in this story! Just like Karoku's dogged search for his beloved wife, Christ, the great "hound of heaven," will never cease from His hunt. He has kept all your tears in His bottle, and He will bring you back to the fold. When all your doubts and insecurities melt away, you too will stand regally and confident before the Lord. I pray the information in this book will be one of the means Christ uses to accomplish just that.

Before continuing to the next chapter, be sure to complete the chapter assignment. Remember, this is *your* game plan and these chapter assignments are a critical component.

Mindful question

What characteristics and behaviors exhibited by Karoku's wife resonated most with your own relationship with God and your life as a Christian? Be specific in your answer.

2

GAME PLAN–PHASE 2: PLAYER IDENTIFICATION

IDENTIFYING THE SOURCES FOR THE OBSTACLES TO ASSURANCE

If you know neither the enemy nor yourself,
you will succumb in every battle.
—Sun Tzu, *The Art of War*

In phase 1 of our game plan, we gathered important contextual information. As part of this initial phase, the unfortunate prevalence of those who struggle to experience the assurance of salvation was established. The scriptural charge to pursue assurance because of its inherent importance was also confirmed. Having laid that foundation, it is time to begin focus on the primary components of our game plan for assurance.

In a football game plan, after giving our team a big picture view of their opponent, and the ramifications of the game (phase 1), we next address the individual players they will be facing. In gathering this information, we use the same thorough approach as we did in phase 1.

To accurately assess the opposing players, coaches look at a variety of metrics. The process begins by identifying the opponents' starting lineup, along with their key backups. We record their physi-cal measurables (heights, weights, athletic ability, etc.). As we exam-ine their top players, we note the level of experience each has in a starting role. Their age and year (sophomore, junior, etc.) are also determined. We continue this identification process until we have a complete profile for each key player of the opposing team.

As coaches, we also engage in "self-scouting." We self-scout our own players in similar fashion as we do our opponents. The pur-pose for this, is to determine favorable and unfavorable matchups that exist with our opponent. Though football is a team sport, these individual matchups greatly influence the outcome of the game and therefore must be accounted for in our game plan.

In our game plan for assurance, we will also "self-scout" to understand the reasons for our own struggles. Only after those caus-ative factors have been identified can we recognize why our specific struggles were exploited and be able to shore up those weaknesses against future assaults on our assurance.

Thus, the strategic place to begin phase 2 of our game plan is to identify the common methods Satan has used repeatedly through the ages to rob a person of his or her assurance. In keeping with the football game plan theme, that's akin to knowing his "players."

Identifying the major sources for the obstacles of assurance

So what are the root causes for assurance-doubt? It is critical to correctly recognize and understand them. For, as one begins to understand the major obstacles to assurance, the process of under-standing and soberly assessing oneself also begins. Accurate assess-ment of both is required for a believer to gain full assurance. As Sun Tzu said, "If you know the enemy and know yourself, you need not fear the result of a hundred battles."

Many people have no idea why they struggle to win the assur-ance of their salvation. All they know is the nagging fear and accus-ing thoughts associated with its absence. Some resign themselves to the notion that assurance will never be part of their faith experi-ence. Others gradually disconnect from God and other believers as the mental and emotional strain mount. "They know neither the enemy nor themselves," and accept defeat, or declare a "truce," trying to avoid the subject altogether. As has been shown, the Bible will endorse neither defeat nor compromise in this battle.

Make no mistake, this is a battle, and the stakes are high. Through the centuries, struggles with assurance has been one of Satan's main weapons to defeat and devour Christians. Not surprisingly, it's a battle many are losing even today. They are losing with no idea how to win.

Like it or not, as a Christian we are engaged in a spiritual battle. We each have our own cross to bear. Struggles with assurance can be an exceedingly fierce battle—and heavy timber to carry. Nevertheless, it's time to get back in the fight; and to pick up your cross again. However, this time you will fight smart! This time you have a game plan!

To begin discussion on identifying the causative hindrances to the assurance of salvation, it is fitting to return to the Westminster Confession of Faith.

> True believers may have the assurance of their salvation divers ways shaken, diminished, and intermitted; as, by negligence in preserving of it; by falling into some special sin, which woundeth the conscience, and grieveth the Spirit; by some sudden or vehement temptation; by God's withdrawing the light of his countenance, and suffering even such as fear him to walk in darkness, and to have no light: yet are they never utterly destitute of that seed of God, and life of faith, that love of Christ, and the brethren, that sincerity of heart and conscience of duty, out of which, by the operation of the Spirit, this assurance may in due time be revived, and by the

which, in the mean time, they are supported from utter despair.[12]

The *Confession* identifies six separate possibilities that play a significant role in undermining one's assurance. The first two concern the living of a disobedient life, which the divines refer to as "*negligence*" and "*falling into some special sin.*" Next, and apparently as a direct result of the first two, the divines identify the emotions as the causative agent in robbing one's assurance. This is denoted as "*wounding the conscience*" and "*grieving the Spirit.*"

The fifth reason is described as a "*sudden or vehement temptation,*" which can overwhelm one's mental faculties. Like a moon trapped in orbit by the great mass of its planet, the force and unexpected occurrence of such wicked thoughts captures one's mind. Consequently, such thoughts and temptations seem impossible to escape. The divines were very insightful to include this as a reason for doubt, as we shall see in later chapters.

Regarding the mind, however, the divines do not identify ignorance or misunderstanding of biblical teaching regarding salvation, as an underlining obstacle, though they clearly state correct theology in prior sections. Evidently, they assumed that knowledge was known and believed, or they did not see its lack as a causative hindrance. It was perhaps a critical omission, as many at the time were influenced by a variety of views regarding assurance. Latham is helpful here.

> Rome denied that it was possible to have certainty of ultimate salvation in this life apart from special revelation or the pronouncement of the church… Within the Reformed churches, there was discussion and disagreement, as to whether the assurance was, as Calvin described it, a normal aspect of saving faith, or whether it came after justification… In the Arminian con-

---

[12] Westminster Assembly, *The Westminster Confession of Faith: (With Poof Texts).* (Glasgow; Free Presbyterian Publications, 1976), chapter 18, section 4.

troversy, election and definite atonement supported assurance, while the weaker views of the
Remonstrants undermined it.[13]

The sixth and final reason the WCF identifies for assurance-doubt is referred to as, *"God withdrawing the light of his counsel."* Latham affirms that "spiritual desertion" was a familiar theme
in Puritan Literature. It also was an important concern in their own
ministries, as many of the divines were pastors of their own flock.[14]
Most today would have no idea what is meant by the term "spiritual
desertion." However, we have all experienced times when God has felt
distant to us and that our prayers were bouncing off heavens of brass.
This can be a very distressing experience for those amid great trials
of life. Certainly King David, Martin Luther, and Charles Spurgeon
would agree! Because of its confusing and disconcerting effect on the
mind, it is appropriate to place this final cause for lack of assurance
also within the realm of one's thoughts. Again, the divines displayed
great insight not only for including this as a causative reason for
assurance-doubt but also in the order they placed it—that is, after a
"sudden or vehement temptation." Indeed, we shall see in chapter 9
the wisdom of the divines for listing their entire list of reasons for a
lack of assurance in the order that they did.

To summarize, the WCF describe three general categories that
are causative reasons for struggles with assurance. These are in relation to one's walk as a believer (actions), one's emotions, and lastly
one's mind (thoughts).

Classifying the major obstacles to assurance

As stated, the WCF is a remarkable work still relevant for
today, but what additions to the topic of assurance have contemporary preachers and theologians offered? There have been a host of

---

[13] Robert Letham, *The Westminster Assembly: Reading Its Theology in Historical
Context* (Phillipsburg; P&R Publishing, 2009), 284.

[14] Ibid., 287.

books, articles and papers written on the subject over the past few decades. If you prefer video, a simple YouTube search will provide numerous sermons on the topic by leading pastors from all over the globe. Obviously, it's impossible to examine all this recent material. However, not too long-ago John MacArthur wrote an excellent book on assurance, which was followed up several years later by an equally exceptional work by Joel Beeke. Both authors include sections highly relevant to the continued development of our game plan, which necessitates a closer look into their work.

Each author includes discussion on the major reasons people struggle to gain the assurance of their salvation. Compiled below are the various obstacles to assurance identified by MacArthur[15] and Beeke[16].

REASONS FOR ASSURANCE-DOUBT

MacArthur	Beeke
Strong legalistic preaching.	History and present experience with sin.
Guilt (difficulty accepting the concept of forgiveness).	False conception of God's character and His Gospel.
Ignorance of the mode of salvation.	Confusion of justification and sanctification.
Uncertainty to the exact time of their salvation.	Failure to profess Christ publicly.
Unrealistic expectations regarding temptation.	Disobedience and backsliding.
Unrealistic expectations regarding trials.	Ignorance of satisfying evidences of grace (Matthew 5:6; Galatians 5:22, 23; 1 John 3:14).

---

[15] John MacArthur, *Saved without a Doubt: Being Sure of Your Salvation* (Colorado Springs; Victor Books, 1992), 111–125.

[16] Joel R. Beeke, Knowing and Growing in Assurance of Faith (Fearn, Ross-shire; Christian Focus Publications, 2017), 25–41.

Fleshly living.	Possessing a doubting or negative disposition (having emotions that tip quickly one way or another).
Disobedience.	Conversion in early childhood or gradual conversion (some can't remember the exact moment of conversion).
	Looking for the wrong kind of experience (looking for an extra-biblical mystical experience).
	Lack of acknowledging or remembering what God has done prior in your life.
	Being attacked by Satan (in our mind, will, and emotions).

Upon close analysis, the three broad categories for assurance obstacles identified within the WCF (thoughts, actions, and emotions) are also present within the lists provided by MacArthur and Beeke. Thus, all struggles with assurance originate from some deficiency or dysfunction within our thoughts, emotions, and actions. In other words, the opponents' starting lineup has been identified and confirmed. Our game plan is taking shape!

Equally important, we are beginning the process of disciplining our minds to dispassionately examine the problem of assurance-doubt. Moreover, breaking down the problem of assurance into its basic parts makes it easier to understand the issue in general. Without this knowledge you won't be able to see the forest for the trees. As a result, you may waste valuable time and experience needless pain moving from one battle to another and implementing failed strategies in your quest for assurance.

Finally, insights into one's own life experiences also emerge when a person can correctly identify their own reasons for struggling with assurance. The process of, "knowing your enemy and yourself," is the way in which a person ultimately gains victory in the pursuit of assurance.

The table on pages 24–25 is helpful in correctly categorizing common hindrances of assurance identified by all three sources we have examined. It's important for a person who lacks assurance to inspect the reasons for other believers' doubts. It's helpful to see that they are not alone in their struggle, and as has already been noted, looking for obstacles that personally resonate will lead to accurate assessment of one's own causes for doubt.

For example, after reading MacArthur's list your attention may have been drawn to the submission of, "strong legalistic preaching" which I placed in the "Emotions" category. As you think more deeply about this you may begin to realize how your own experiences in an overly strict family or church has negatively impacted your ability to experience assurance. Perhaps a reason from Beeke's list resonates. You may have come to Christ as a young child, and you can't remember the circumstances of your conversion; as a result, you lack assurance that you're truly saved now.

As you read through this list, as well as the rest of the information presented in this book, ask the Holy Spirit to reveal the causative reasons for your struggles with assurance. Remember the importance of "self-scouting"! Therefore, within the table is a column to fill in the reasons you think may be contributing to your own lack of assurance. Don't worry if you can't identify anything specific yet, as you continue through the book, the Holy Spirit will reveal those hidden things (1 Corinthians 2:10). After completing your self-scout assessment, be sure to answer the "Mindful Question" before moving on to chapter 3.

Sources	Thoughts	Emotions	Actions
WCF	sudden or vehement temptation; God withdrawing the light of His counsel (Spiritual desertion).	wounding the conscience and grieving the Spirit.	negligence in preserving assurance; falling into some special sin.

MacArthur	ignorance of the mode of salvation; uncertainty to the exact time of salvation; unrealistic expectations regarding temptation; unrealistic expectations regarding trials;	guilt (difficulty accepting the concept of forgiveness); strong legalistic preaching;	fleshly living; disobedience.
Beeke	false conception of God's character and His Gospel; confusion of justification and sanctification; ignorance of satisfying evidences of grace; conversion in early childhood or gradual conversion; looking for the wrong kind of experience; lack of acknowledging or remembering what God has done prior in your life; being attacked by Satan.	possessing a doubting or negative disposition— controlled by swings of emotions; being attacked by Satan.	history and present experience with sin; failure to profess Christ publicly; disobedience and backsliding; being attacked by Satan.
Self-Scout			

Mindful question

The WCF explained that a "sudden or vehement temptation," which I placed in the "Thoughts" category, can be a cause for struggles with assurance. Why do you think this is true?

3

GAME PLAN–PHASE 3:
SCHEMES AND TENDENCIES

RECOGNIZING THE SYNERGISM WITHIN
THE OBSTACLES TO ASSURANCE

The whole is greater than the sum of its parts.

—Aristotle

In the previous chapter, it was shown that the common obstacles to assurance of salvation are rooted in our own thoughts, emotions, and actions. As the old comic strip quipped, "We have met the enemy and he is us"! This is vital to comprehend, as many people who struggle with assurance may believe that God is to blame for their struggles.

I can remember asking God why He put verses like "the blasphemy of the Holy Spirit" in the Bible when He knew many people such as myself would wreck their assurance obsessing over them. Even the great John Bunyan had similar concerns.

> I would also think that there only seemed to
> be three or four Scriptures against me, and I wondered if God would overlook those and save me.
> Other times I would think how much I might be

26

> comforted if it were not for these three or four
> verses, and I could not keep myself from wishing
> at times that those verses were not in the Bible.[17]

As you might expect, I got no immediate answer to my question. However, the Holy Spirit would gradually reveal, as I became able to bear it (John 16:12–14), the answers to much deeper and more poignant questions. Indeed, this book is a compilation of those answers. So with that in mind, let's continue with the game plan!

I mentioned that football game plans are developed in a general to specific format. Once all the baseline information on our opponent, game, and players are gathered (phases 1 and 2), we begin the process of recognizing their schemes and tendencies. This is phase 3 of the game plan.

Football schemes refer to how the opponent positions their players on the field and what they do from those different positions. For example, we look at the opponents' favorite offensive formations and defensive fronts. We determine their top run and pass plays on offense, as well as their favorite coverages and blitz packages on defense. We continue to gather this schematic data before looking at their tendencies.

Tendencies refer to when, how and why teams do certain things. For example, what do they do in short yardage situations, third and long, and other down and distance scenarios? How do they attack certain defensive fronts, and defend different offensive formations? We continue to analyze all their tendencies until a clear pattern emerges.

In phase 3 we also self-scout our own schemes and tendencies. We do this to predict how our opponent will attack us and prepare for those possible scenarios in our game plan. Another important purpose for conducting a self-scout is to make sure we are not an easy team to figure out and expose. Likewise, the concept of identifying schemes and tendencies and conducting self-scouts is extremely important for our assurance game plan as we shall see.

---

[17] Ibid., 89.

The scheme of synergy

Much effort has been expended in the identification of the three general categories for the obstacles to assurance of salvation (thoughts, emotions, and actions) during phase 2 of our game plan. Now that these general categories for the obstacles to assurance have been identified, the next step in our game plan is to analyze and understand them.

How can these three vastly different aspects of an individual be the cause of struggles with assurance? In other words, what scheme is being employed in the interaction of one's thoughts, emotions, and actions that rob a person of assurance?

I will tell you now and demonstrate it later through the Word and scientific research that the scheme we are hunting is the phenomena of synergy. Synergy is the invisible force that ties our thoughts, emotions, and actions together, and powerfully converges them to a positive or negative end. In football terminology, this convergence for good or ill, can be understood as the "tendency" for the "scheme" of synergy.

Understanding the synergy that exists between our thoughts, emotions and actions is critical for everyone to grasp, not just those who lack assurance. If you take anything away from this book let it be that. Indeed, a main premise of our game plan is that this inherent synergy not only explains how struggles with assurance begin, but also why they are very difficult to overcome. Given its great importance, we need to fully unpack what is meant by the term synergy before continuing with our game plan.

Synergy comes from the Greek word "συνεργός" or "synergos." The prefix "syn-" means "with" or "together," and the suffix "-erg" refers to "work" or "labor." However, like its definition the word itself is more than just the sum of its parts. It carries with it the idea of working together in a process to bring something to completeness.[18]

---

[18] James Strong, The New Strong's Exhaustive Concordance of the Bible (Thomas Nelson Publishers, Nashville, 1990), 86.

The full meaning of the word expresses two related ideas. First, the necessity of working together to bring something to fullness or completion. Secondly, synergy implies that the combined action or work has a total effect greater than the sum of its parts—a "two plus two equals five" effect.

Examples of synergy can be seen in nature in what biologists call symbiotic relationships. For example, in Africa, there is a bird called the oxpecker that has a unique relationship with zebras and rhinos. The hide of a zebra and rhinoceros can get infested with fleas and ticks. The oxpecker hitches a ride on the backs of these animals, feeding on these insects and ridding their hides of these parasites in the process. It's a win-win situation for all. The oxpecker gets an easy meal and the zebra and rhino get relief from the constant harassment of these pests. The relationship produces even more benefits. The oxpecker has extremely keen eyesight and makes a very loud caw when predators are approaching, thus alerting the zebra and rhino of approaching danger. By riding on the back of a rhino or a nine-hun-dred-pound zebra, natural predators of the oxpecker, have to look elsewhere for their next meal! The synergistic relationship between these three animals greatly increases their odds for survival.

The business world is constantly striving for synergy as well. I have spent over thirty years in the pharmaceutical and biotech indus-try. During my career, I have seen and experienced many mergers of different companies. Separate companies join because the combined human ingenuity, technological resources, and revenue stream of the newly merged company increases its chances to remain viable and profitable.

Synergy is the highly sought prize in the arts as well. As a foot-ball coach, I believe being on time is late, so to my wife's chagrin, I like to arrive to our destination fifteen minutes early (at least). So of course, the first time we went to the symphony together we got there well before the orchestra began. As we sat in our seats listening to the various musicians warming up and tuning their instruments, I was struck by how inharmonious they sounded. However, when the conductor arrived on stage, and the performance began, those same instruments were now being played in perfect tempo and melody.

That is synergy. It's achieved when the poet chooses the perfect words and arranges them in the correct structure in keeping with the theme of the poem, or when the artist constructs a masterpiece with layers of a perfectly chosen colors.

Finally, synergy can also be seen in the Bible. The word "συνεργός" (*synergos*) is used thirteen times in the New Testament and almost exclusively by the apostle Paul. He uses the term to describe his fellow workers (Timothy, Titus, Priscilla, Aquilla, etc.). In using this particular word, Paul is drawing our attention to both aspects of the definition of synergy. Namely, the necessity of working together for a result greater than the sum of its parts.

The use of the word intimates how God multiplied the collective efforts of Paul and his fellow workers in the Gospel. Paul illustrates this synergy in 1 Corinthians 3:6, "I planted, Apollos watered, but God gave the growth." The Gospel of Mark records the same, "And they went forth, and preached everywhere, the Lord working with them, and confirming the word with signs following. Amen" (Mark 16:20 KJV).

All of these are examples of positive synergism. However, there is such a thing as negative synergism—a "two plus two equals three" scenario. We often describe negative synergy with phrases like, "the perfect storm," "snowballing" or the "ripple effect." Such references are not surprising, as negative synergism can be seen in many natural catastrophes.

A classic example of negative synergism in nature is the tsunami. A tsunami is initially caused by large and sudden disturbance in the ocean. This disturbance is caused by an underwater earthquake or volcanic eruption. The source of these disturbances are oftentimes hundreds of miles away from where the tsunami finally makes landfall. The tsunami wave starts off extremely fast but is only a meter or two in height. A person would hardly feel it pass by at this initial stage. However, as it approaches shore it slows down rises to monstrous heights and devastates everything in its path as it hits shore.

In literature, harmful synergy is depicted in the genre of tragedy. In such stories, the hero is brought down through a series of unfortunate events by his one fatal flaw. As the story of the tragedy progresses, the hero's enemies methodically expose and exploit his "Achilles' heel" until he is defeated. Certainly, the biblical account of the life of Samson is a prime example.

I mentioned that corporate mergers were a favored method for engineering positive synergy in the business world. However, sometimes companies just are not a good match. Instead of increased profits, the result of these "bad chemistry" mergers are restructuring, downsizing, and layoffs. I've been through my share of them as well!

Thus, the tendency for the scheme of synergy can be either positive or negative. Synergy is the mechanism responsible for a person's thoughts to be lucid and clear or confused and muddled. A person's emotional state is also regulated by synergy. Whether you're given to stoicism or anxiousness, synergy plays a key role. Synergy also influences our actions, underpinning the well-ordered and structured life, or the exacerbation of one already frantic out of control.

Whether one struggles with assurance of salvation or not, synergy is the common denominator. For the former, negative synergy is operative; and for the latter, who have no assurance-doubt, positive synergy is the tendency in force. Thus, the importance of understanding the positive or negative synergy of thought, emotion, and action is critical to our game plan.

As mentioned, for those who lack assurance, the negative synergy of their thoughts, emotions, and actions is the operative tendency—the "two plus two equals three" scenario. Instead of producing lucidity, confidence and stability, the confluence of the thoughts, emotions, and actions in a believer who lacks assurance, produces doubt, fear, and wavering.

Hopefully, I have done an adequate job of describing what is fully meant by synergy. You'll recall that there are two aspects to the definition of synergy. First is the concept of two or more "things" working closely together to bring a desired end to completion. The second aspect is that the desired end, whether good or bad, is greater than the sum of its parts. Now we need to demonstrate how the synergy of our thoughts, emotions and actions fulfill both aspects of that definition. To do so, we will examine Scriptural and scientific evidence.

Scriptural proof of synergy

Below are just a few passages of Scripture that show the close relationship between our thoughts, emotions, and actions. I will designate those sections for the sake of ready identification. The sections that depict our *actions* will be designated with the superscript "A," emotions will be designated the superscript "E," and "T" will designate references to thoughts.

Like any coach worth his salt, I will also provide brief explanations noting the synergy that exists between each of the three aspects. Hundreds of scriptural examples could have been chosen to show this relationship, but for now we will take a close look at only four passages.

1. **(What you have learned and received and heard and seen in me)**^{T}—**(practice these things)**^{A}, and **(the God of peace)**^{E} will be with you. (Philippians 4:9)

There's an old saying in medicine, "see one, do one, teach one." The point is, sometimes you don't know something well enough to competently teach it, until you do it yourself. This is the main thrust of our first example from the book of Philippians.

In this passage, Paul instructs his readers to think about his teachings, remember them, meditate on them. Let them take root in their mind. Not only his teachings, but also how he conducted his life. His work ethic, humility, and his treatment of others. Paul then tells them to do or practice those same things. The result of thinking and acting correctly according to Paul would be that the God of peace would be with them. Notice that Paul did not say the God of power, or the God of mercy, or even the God of grace would be with them, but the God of peace.

This passage clearly shows the synergy that exists between our thoughts, emotions and actions. When thinking and behavior are aligned with truth, your emotions follow suit, for the God of peace will be with you. When the God of peace is with you, the sum is indeed greater than the parts!

"See one, do one, teach one," those old country doctors were right; there are certain things you won't really know or be convinced of, until you do it.

> 2. The Jews therefore marveled, saying, "How is it that this man has learning, when he has never studied?" So Jesus answered them, "My teaching is not mine, but his who sent me. If **(anyone's will is)**ᴱ **(to do God's will)** ᴬ, **(he will know whether the teaching is from God)**ᵀ or whether I am speaking on my own authority. The one who speaks on his own authority seeks his own glory; but the one who seeks the glory of him who sent him is true, and in him there is no falsehood. (John 7:17)

To grasp the significance of Christ's response to the Jews we must consider the circumstances surrounding this encounter. The immediate context of this verse is when Jesus was teaching in the temple courts during the Feast of Tabernacles. However, the Jews were still angry that Jesus had healed a paralyzed man on the Sabbath a few days earlier (John 5), but now that irritation turns to amazement as they listen to His teachings.

As we examine the above passage, it is important to first hear what Jesus' response was to the Jews' anger for healing the man on the Sabbath a few days prior. Jesus said, "But I know that you do not have the love of God within you. I have come in my Father's name, and you do not receive me. If another comes in his own name, you will receive him. How can you believe, when you receive glory from one another and do not seek the glory that comes from the only God?" (John 5:42–44).

As mentioned, in just a few days' time, these same religious leaders who were angry at His healing practices, were now marveling at His teaching ability! However, Jesus is not so fickle, and He gives a remarkably similar and astute answer in John 7:17 as He did in John 5.

In John 7:17, Christ in effect tells the unbelieving Jews that it is impossible for their minds to think correctly about Him. Why? Because the desires of their hearts were corrupt, which led to corrupt actions. These Jews did not understand Christ's teaching because they did not love God, nor seek His glory. They loved the praise of men, and the actions of their lives were continuously bent on seeking their own glory (Matthew 23:5–7), proving the dullness of their mind. Here Jesus clearly links the prerequisites for correct thinking about Himself—namely a pure heart that loves God and seeks to obey Him in actions.

Below is a bonus verse I will include from the book of Psalms that reveals this same synergy. See if you can accurately place the appropriate superscript with regards to the presence of thoughts, emotions, and actions. To help, I will separate the key sections of the verse.

(**"The fear of the Lord)** is the beginning of wisdom: **(a good understanding have all they) (that do his commandments:")** (Psalm 111:10a).

3. (...**that their hearts may be encouraged, being knit together in love)**[E] **(to reach all the riches of full assurance of understanding and the knowledge of God's mystery, which is Christ, in whom are hidden all the treasures of wisdom and knowledge)**.[T] I say this in order that no one may delude you with plausible arguments. For though I am absent in body, yet I am with you in spirit, rejoicing to see (**your good order and the firmness of your faith in Christ)**.[A] (Colossians 2:2–5)

Ironically, this third passage addresses the same topic of our game plan—the assurance of salvation. Although Paul had not visited the Colossian church, their minister, Epaphras, told Paul all about them, and shared with Paul how his congregation was being assaulted by Gnostic heresies.

The word gnostic means, "to know" and these heretics were suggesting that the Gospel Paul and Epaphras taught was incomplete. These Gnostic teachers espoused that there were deeper, extra-biblical "mysteries" necessary for salvation. As a result of these troubling heresies, the believers in Colossae lost their assurance of salvation. In Paul's prayer to address this assault on their assurance, he shows the close connection between our thoughts, emotions, and actions (Colossians 2:2–5).

Paul prays first that their hearts may once again be encouraged and filled with love, as opposed to fear. Once that fear was dispelled, their minds would again be able to meditate fully and unencumbered on the truth of who Jesus actually is, as opposed to some cryptic and cultish mystery. Paul was confident that as their thoughts turned to Christ, the full assurance of their salvation would return. Paul was equally sure that the emotion of love, and correct thinking on Christ, would occasion him to see their disciplined life of obedience on display. In both Pauline passages, he clearly links how our thoughts, emotions, and actions are intertwined.

> 4. Grace and **(peace be yours in abundance)**[E] **(through the knowledge of God and of Jesus our Lord)**.[T] His divine power has given us **(everything we need for a godly life)**[A] **(through our knowledge of him)**[T] who called us by his own glory and goodness. (2 Peter 1:2–3)

In this last example, Peter prays for the recipients of his letter to experience genuine abundant peace, through the knowledge of God and Jesus Christ. Remember that the second aspect of synergism is that the end result is greater than the sum of its parts. Peter is expressing that phenomenon here, as noted author and pastor, Chuck Smith explains.

> Grace and peace, typical greetings. But here Peter is praying really that they be multiplied. And how are they multiplied? The more you know God, the more you know Jesus Christ, the more you experience and are blessed by the grace of God and as the result, experience the peace of God. Grace and peace be multiplied. How? Through your knowledge of God and of Jesus Christ.[19]

In this first part of the verse, Peter links the emotion of peace with the correct understanding of Christ. In the last section of the verse, Peter was confident that as their knowledge of God increased, so would their ability to live a godly life.

Recall that in both Pauline passages we examined, the order of impact was different in each. In the passage from Colossians, the order presented is emotion-thought-action, and in the Philippians passage, the order is thought-action-emotion. Thus, we see the order of connection has no bearing on the result. In other words, whether it is our thoughts, emotions, or actions that serve as the initial impetus, the other two will be affected.

At this point, you may be wondering why I would point this out. Trust me, this is not evidence of the overly analytical mind of a football coach! There has been much debate in medical and psychological circles regarding which aspect (thought/emotion/action) comes first.

Some experts are convinced that our emotions initiate this connection with our thoughts and actions. As evidence for their position, they note that sensory input must first enter the emotional cen-

---

[19] Chuck Smith, "Verse by Verse Study on 2 Peter 1–3 (C2000)." Blue Letter Bible. (June 1, 2005). Web. January 25, 2023. https://www.blueletterbible.org/Comm/smith_chuck/c2000_2Pe/2Pe_001.cfm.

ters of the brain before reaching the areas responsible for conscious thought. Others adhere to more intuitive evidence, where thoughts produce emotions, which in turn drive one to action. Finally, there are proponents of behavioral therapy that stress the importance of action as the main driver of emotions and thoughts.

Despite the disagreement on the ordinary order of this connection, all acknowledge that a change in any of the three will impact the other two. In other words, kick-starting the cycle of synergy (for positive or negative results), will still occur by the initial impact of either one's thoughts, emotions, or actions. This fact is a critical concept to understand for our game plan and will be developed fully in our discussion of the five obstacles to the assurance of salvation.

In conclusion, the synergistic connection between our thoughts, emotions, and actions described in the Scriptures are apparent when one becomes aware of and looks for it. The verses that display this connection seem to hide in plain sight throughout the Bible. Indeed, many verses could have been chosen and developed to show this association. Understanding this relationship, and seeing it verified in the Word, is vital for a person struggling with assurance.

Before we continue game-planning to see how this "scheme and tendency" is verified by current medical and psychological research, I have a mid-chapter assignment for you. Please complete this, before finishing the rest of the chapter.

Mindful question

To solidify what we just learned; I want you to examine the following passage. First, set the passage in proper context. Second, note the references to thought, emotion and action and explain the synergy you observe.

> They are darkened in their understanding, alienated from the life of God because of the ignorance that is in them, due to their hardness of heart.

They have become callous and have given themselves up to sensuality, greedy to practice every kind of impurity. (Ephesians 4:18–19)

Scientific proof of synergy

Hopefully you did well with your assignment and are now convinced of the biblical evidence for the synergy of thought, emotion, and action. However, now it's time to show how this synergy is supported scientifically.

The interaction between a person's thoughts, emotions and actions is a well-documented phenomenon in psychology. Aaron T. Beck, of the University of Pennsylvania, is the psychiatrist who pioneered the management of various types of psychological disorders based on this underlying premise. His distinctive approach of addressing the relationship between thoughts, emotions and actions helped form the basis for what is now known as cognitive behavioral therapy. His daughter Judith, an accomplished psychiatrist as well, summarizes the basic tenets of this approach.

These adaptations have changed the focus, technology, and length of treatment, but the theoretical assumptions themselves remained constant. In a nutshell, the cognitive model proposes that distorted or dysfunctional thinking (which influences the patient's mood and behavior) is common to all psychological disturbances.[20]

Dr. Jeffrey Schwartz, MD, is one of the foremost experts on obsessive-compulsive disorder, and proponent of CBT. In his book, *Brain Lock,* Schwartz also confirms this interaction, "It's not how you feel that counts, but what you do that counts. Because when you do the right things feelings tend to improve as a matter of course...

---

[20] Judith S. Beck, *Cognitive Therapy: Basics and Beyond* (New York; The Guilford Press, 1995), 1.

Focus your attention on the mental and physical actions that will improve your life."[21] Here Schwartz, affirms the synergistic relationship between our thoughts, emotions, and actions by stating how making a change in one or two areas will influence the other(s).

This understanding of the synergy of thoughts, emotions and actions which is fundamental to the cognitive behavioral model is the major reason for the success of this therapy. In fact, CBT has surpassed Freudian psychoanalysis as a favored modality to treat a majority of psychological disorders. That said, even psychoanalysis seeks to determine meaning from a person's thoughts, actions, and feelings, albeit from the unconscious mind.

Like the scriptural references, confirmations of the synergy between thought, emotion, and action are replete in scientific literature. Though all psychological therapies differ in their methods, this synergistic connection is fundamental to all theories and modalities.

At this point, we can conclude that both the Bible and medical research has verified the synergistic connection between thought, emotion, and action. As we progress through this book, proof of this connection will continue to be a dominant theme. However, now we need to address exactly how this connection occurs.

Much of my formal education and training has been the field of biology and medicine. So I like to understand how biological systems and processes work. Therefore, when I first became aware of the synergy that we have been discussing, I was curious to know if there was a biological mechanism responsible for it. Turns out there is, and Dr. Schwartz explains in physiologic terms how the inherent synergism that exists between our thoughts, emotions, and actions (which can result in either positive, or self-destructive outcomes), occurs.

> The answer lies in Hebb's law, which states that where nerve cells are activated in the same pattern repeatedly, they eventually form a brain circuit. Once the circuit is established, the

---

[21] Jeffrey Schwartz, *Brain Lock* (New York; Harper Collins, 2016), introduction xiix.

brain areas involved in the circuit automatically respond in the same way every time a similar situation arises. This causes the circuit to become stronger-and it is how habits, such as a riding a bike, learning to drink when stressed, or relearning how to walk after a stroke, are created and maintained.[22]

This cyclical physiologic dynamic described by Schwartz is present in other biological systems. One example are processes called positive feedback loops. Positive feedback loops are found in processes that need to be pushed to a completion, a classic example being childbirth.

In childbirth, the baby's head presses on the cervix—the bottom of the uterus, through which the baby must emerge—and activates neurons to the brain. The neurons send a signal that leads to release of the hormone oxytocin from the pituitary gland. Oxytocin increases uterine contractions, and thus pressure on the cervix. This causes the release of even more oxytocin and produces even stronger contractions. This positive feedback loop continues until the baby is born.[23]

Below is a graphic representation of the positive feedback loop for both childbirth and a visual representation of the interplay between thoughts, emotions, and actions often used by cognitive therapists. I will refer to the latter representation as a "TEA graph" moving forward. Think of this TEA graph as a visual aid to add to our game plan.

As we work through the information in this book the TEA graph will be gradually amended to depict how our struggles with assurance begin and progress as well as to provide a vivid picture of all the conditions necessary for genuine assurance. I am a visual per-

---

[22] Jeffrey Schwartz and Rebecca Gladding, *You Are Not Your Brain* (London; Penguin Books, 2012), 62–63.

[23] J. Gordon Betts et al, Anatomy and Physiology (Rice University, 1999–2022), 1.5 Homeostasis https://creativecommons.org/licenses/by/4.0/.

son and have found this tool to be very helpful to graphically depict the factors that impact a person's assurance.

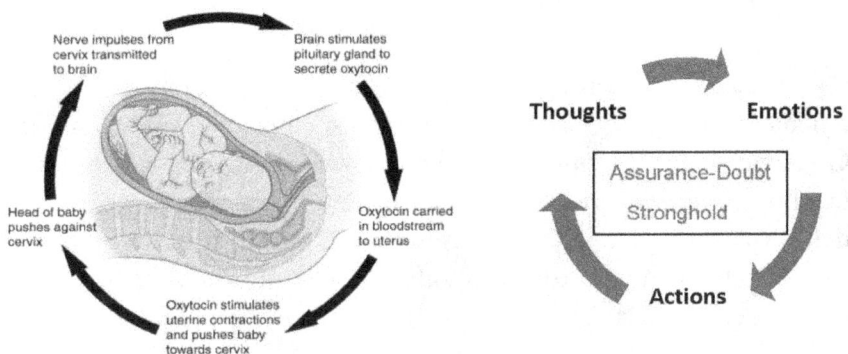

As mentioned, the main premise of this book is that the synergistic interaction that exists between our thoughts, emotions and actions explains the difficulty for believers to experience the assurance of their salvation. This insidious relationship is also the reason struggles with assurance can become a profound and long-lasting problem.

The process is like the positive feedback loop noted in childbirth. For example, let's look at a scenario with the tendency for negative synergy, that will produce an undesirable outcome, such as assurance-doubt.

Our thoughts influence our emotions, which in turn impacts our actions. Our behaviors then reinforce and perpetuate the original thoughts that first generated the cycle. Via the mechanism of Hebb's law, each time this cycle of thought, emotion and action occurs it grows in power and persistence.

Remember this cycle can start with our emotions or actions as well. Regardless of the original impetus, if this negative cycle of synergy is left to continue unaltered, the result will not be the equivalent of a beautiful baby, but what Paul would describe as a "stronghold" (2 Corinthians 10:4). In our case, the stronghold of assurance-doubt. Therefore, before moving on in our game plan, we must discuss the very serious nature of spiritual strongholds and the weapons necessary to tear them down.

Mindful question

Describe two situations in your own life that demonstrated the scheme of synergy between your thoughts, emotions, and behaviors. Give two examples, one where the operative tendency was negative (an unpleasant experience), and the other where the operative tendency was positive (a pleasant experience). In both situations, discuss the thoughts you had, the emotions you felt, and the specific behaviors you engaged in.

4

THE VENUE: SPIRITUAL STRONGHOLDS

Welcome to Death Valley, where opponents' dreams come to die!
                                        —Ed Orgeron, LSU head football coach

Spiritual strongholds

In the opening chapter of this book, I mentioned the impact the venue has in determining the outcome of a football game, and that this concept was also critical to our game plan for gaining the assurance of salvation. In fact, I said this topic was so important, that an entire chapter would be needed to fully explain its significance. Moreover, the information I presented in each of the first three chapters was done so to bring us to this essential issue in our game plan, so a brief review is in order.

In chapter 1, Sinclair Ferguson laid our ultimate goal before us by clearly defining the assurance of salvation. As part of this initial phase of our game plan, I also discussed important contextual issues regarding the lack of assurance. In chapter 2 (phase 2) we identified our thoughts, emotions, and actions as the three common denominators for struggles with assurance, and in chapter 3 (phase 3) we discussed the synergistic relationship between our thoughts, emotions, and actions and its tendency for either positive or negative results (see table below).

General Causes for Assurance-Doubt	Scheme	Tendency
Thoughts, Emotions, Actions	Synergy	Negative

At the close of the last chapter, I stated that the negative synergy that exists between our thoughts, emotions, and actions can lead to what Paul described as a stronghold.

Thus, the battle for our assurance occurs in a very dangerous "venue" that the Bible identifies as a spiritual stronghold. To be successful in gaining the assurance of salvation, we need to thoroughly understand spiritual strongholds, because that is the stadium, if you will where we must face our opponent.

There is much confusion in the church today surrounding this topic. On the one hand, I have seen spiritual strongholds fantastically portrayed in demonic possession, and on the other hand, they have been trivialized to account for every human vice or personality quirk. No wonder, the topic of spiritual strongholds and warfare gets avoided in most pulpits across the country.

Despite the extreme views, there is most definitely a demonic and human role that is played in the development and defense of spiritual strongholds. Therefore, we cannot avoid the topic, but we must place the subject of spiritual strongholds and spiritual warfare in proper perspective.

First, to understand what spiritual strongholds are, we need to determine what the Bible has to say about strongholds in general. After that important foundation is laid, we will then determine how spiritual strongholds are formed, and the dangers that will be encountered in tearing them down.

Definition of spiritual strongholds

The Greek word for stronghold that Paul uses in 2 Corinthians 10:4 is "ὀχύρωμα" (okh-oo'-ro-mah), and it appears over thirty times in the Bible. Strong defines the word as a "castle, stronghold, or fortress, or simply as anything on which one relies."[24]

There are two basic types of strongholds described in the Bible. One would be a man-made structure, normally found within the protective gates of a city. In ancient times, if the walls of a city were breached by the enemy, the people would retreat as a last resort within the walls of the stronghold. Abimilech's destruction of the Shecemites, who took refuge within the walls of their temple-stronghold, is a prime example.

> So every one of the people cut down his bundle and following Abimelech put it against the stronghold, and they set the stronghold on fire over them, so that all the people of the Tower of Shechem also died, about 1,000 men and women. (Judges 9:49)

Such city-strongholds were scattered throughout the promised land, making it difficult for the children of Israel to drive out their enemies. Israel's early history is characterized by accounts of these strongholds being won and lost as part of the constant battle with the surrounding pagan nations. As Israel became lax in their allegiance to God, their enemies re-gained control of these strategic strongholds. The book of Judges records the specifics of these cyclical battles.

In addition to man-made strongholds, natural strongholds are also common in the Old Testament. These would be difficult to locate and access areas of the wilderness. Such strongholds were found deep within forests, in secret desert caves, or high up in the mountain cliffs. David in his flight from Saul was constantly hiding himself in these natural strongholds (1 Samuel 23:14–24:22).

Therefore, these strongholds, whether natural or man-made were highly prized for the safety, security, and power they provided for their possessors. Ironically, strongholds were also a type of prison

---

[24] "G3794—ochyrōma—Strong's Greek Lexicon (esv)." Blue Letter Bible. Web. 11 Feb, 2023. <https://www.blueletterbible.org/lexicon/g3794/esv/tr/0–1/>.

where people upon entering, sacrificed their freedom, as David understood all too well.

> I cry to you, O LORD; I say, "You are my
> refuge, my portion in the land of the living."
> Attend to my cry, for I am brought very
> low! Deliver me from my persecutors, for they
> are too strong for me!
> Bring me out of prison, that I may give
> thanks to your name! (Psalm 142:5–7a)

Psalm 142 was written by David while he was in the cave of Adullam. This natural stronghold was strategically located on the border of ancient Philistia and Israel. The cave provided David and his band of men safety from the Philistines and from King Saul. Despite the safety the cave provided, David saw it for what it was, a prison (v. 7).

Moreover, David acknowledges that God alone is his refuge (v. 5). No man in Israel's history has spent more time on the run and hiding out in the natural strongholds scattered throughout the land than did David. They served him well, but David never put his trust in them. David saw God as his stronghold and said so often.

> The LORD is a stronghold for the oppressed,
> a stronghold in times of trouble. (Psalm 9:9)

> The LORD is my rock and my fortress and
> my deliverer, my God, my rock, in whom I take
> refuge, my shield, and the horn of my salvation,
> my stronghold. (Psalm 18:2)

> The LORD is my light and my salvation;
> whom shall I fear? The LORD is the stronghold of
> my life; of whom shall I be afraid? (Psalm 27:1)

> The salvation of the righteous is from the
> LORD; he is their stronghold in the time of trou-
> ble. (Psalm 37:39)

> But the LORD has become my stronghold,
> and my God the rock of my refuge. (Psalm 94:22)

> He is my steadfast love and my fortress, my
> stronghold and my deliverer, my shield and he in
> whom I take refuge, who subdues peoples under
> me. (Psalm 144:2)

Despite being a prison of sorts, people took pride in the safety
and security their strongholds supplied. Calvin famously said, "The
human heart is a perpetual idol factory," so it is no surprise that such
strongholds became an instrument of idolatry. As a result, the Old
Testament records several instances where God judges the nations by
destroying their strongholds (Amos 1:7, 10, 12; Isaiah 23:4, 11,14).
Even Israel was not spared this fate.

> For Israel has forgotten his Maker and built
> palaces, and Judah has multiplied fortified cities;
> so I will send a fire upon his cities, and it shall
> devour her strongholds. (Hosea 8:14)

> You have breached all his walls; you have
> laid his strongholds in ruins. (Psalms 89:40)

Dark inaccessible hiding places, impenetrable fortresses used as
tactical footholds, and sources of prideful idolatry: This is the imagery Paul wants the Corinthians to meditate on when he uses the term
stronghold metaphorically. Below is the passage in its entirety.

> For the weapons of our warfare are not of
> the flesh but have divine power to destroy strong-
> holds. We destroy arguments and every lofty

47

> opinion raised against the knowledge of God, and take every thought captive to obey Christ, being ready to punish every disobedience, when your obedience is complete. (2 Corinthians 10:4–6)

Paul wants the Corinthians to understand that the real war we face as Christians begins and resides in our minds. Paul identifies these enemies as "arguments" and "lofty opinions" that oppose the Word of God.

The Greek word for *arguments* Paul uses is λογισμός (logismas), and it carries with it the meaning of a reckoning or reasoning that is hostile to the Christian faith. The Greek word; ὕψωμα (hoop-so-mah), translated as "lofty opinion," refers to an elevated structure or rampart, thus the King James Bible translates "lofty opinion" as "high thing."

When putting these two Greek words together, it becomes apparent why Paul uses the word *stronghold* to describe such idolatrous thoughts. Howson provides further insight into Paul's reasons for using this metaphor, and its particular relevance for the Corinthian believers.

> The "strongholds" are the rock forts, such as those which once bristled along the coast of his native Cilicia and of which he must often have heard when his father told him how they were "pulled down" by the Romans in their wars against the pirates. Those "high things that exalt themselves"—those high eminences of the pride of Nature—occupied in force by hostile troops—had been a familiar experience in many wars throughout Asia Minor, while one of the grandest of all was the Acropolis that towered over Corinth.[25]

---

[25] John S. Howson, *The Metaphors of St. Paul* (London; Hodder and Stoughton, 1883), 34–35.

We have already proved that our thoughts do not exist in a vacuum. Paul understood this as well. So he states that every wicked thought must be taken captive before it can manifest in our attitudes and actions. Every thought we think, every lie we tolerate, that exalts itself against the truth, is one brick, one stone, laid in the construction of a stronghold in our minds. Once laid, these bricks and stones are cemented in place by the negative emotions and attitudes they evoke. This ungodly edifice of wicked lies and destructive emotions is then fiercely guarded and kept by the sinful actions they induce. This is what a spiritual stronghold is in its entirety, and it must be taken and torn down—brick by brick, stone by stone and soldier by soldier.

However, tearing down spiritual strongholds is no easy task. Their location is strategic and tough to access. They are not hidden within the gates of a city, or a secret mountain pass, but deep within our own mind and heart.

As mentioned, spiritual strongholds are heavily fortified. Their high towers and bulwarks are constructed by the lies of the evil one. The most unbecoming aspects of our own character; pride, fear, bitterness, and a host of other woeful passions, serve as the strongest of binding mortars.

Moreover, spiritual strongholds are guarded by formidable foes. For some individuals, these strongholds are protected by garrisons of legalistic behaviors; for others, crack battalions of antinomian license are its defenders. Regardless of what "uniform" these soldiers wear, they are constantly being resupplied and strengthened by wicked influences of the world, the flesh, and the devil (Ephesians 2:2–3a).

Despite the difficulty of tearing down spiritual strongholds, we are commanded to do it. However, before attempting such a difficult assignment, there is more we need to understand about the formation of spiritual strongholds.

Determiners of spiritual strongholds: Dichotomy and dysfunction

How is it possible that a born-again believer could fall prey to the deceitful wickedness of a spiritual stronghold? Doesn't the Bible

49

say that we are no longer enemies of God, that we have been washed of our sin, and are sons and daughters of the Most High? It certainly does! However, there are still ramifications of the fall that also define us. It is the dichotomy that is present in all of us, and the unfortunate dysfunction that is present in some of us, that makes spiritual strongholds possible and extremely difficult to dismantle.

Dichotomy

So what is this dichotomy that makes us susceptible to spiritual attack as well as accomplices in the construction of spiritual strongholds? When we become Christians, we are given a new heavenly nature in Christ. However, the old sinful, earthly, nature from Adam is still present within us. It's true, we are new creatures in Christ, yet we remain fallen creatures, living in a fallen world. The Holy Spirit lives in us, but so does sin. The "new man" and the "old man" coexist. This is the dichotomy.

Satan is quick to take advantage of our divided nature. He incessantly seduces the "old nature," to draw us away from godly thoughts, desires, and disciplines. In addition, this constant enticement by Satan is often accompanied by the willing participation of the sinful nature still present within us (Romans 7:20; James 1:14).

In his classic work, *The Freedom of the Will*, Jonathan Edwards, America's greatest philosopher and theologian came to the simple yet profound conclusion—human beings always choose to do what they are most strongly inclined to do at the time. In other words, man always chooses what he perceives will benefit him most. Too often, the desires of the old man are stronger than those of the new man. It is this dichotomy and spiritual battle that made Paul cry out, "Wretched man that I am! Who will deliver me from this body of death?" (Romans 7:24).

Dysfunction

Compounding this issue is the distinct possibility that individuals who struggle with the assurance of salvation may also have an underlying genetic tendency toward obsessions and compulsions and/or other exacerbating psychological or cultural influences. Such dysfunction is also a ramification of the fall.

It is important to stress, that the causes for the formation of spiritual strongholds, namely the substitution of falsehood for truth, is the same for those suffering from mental dysfunction. However, the manner and motivations for the initial formation of spiritual strongholds is vastly different, and often out of their control. The same can be said of the resulting effect on the emotions and behaviors. For this reason, a spiritual stronghold that exists within a believer with certain mental dysfunctions poses unique challenges. Nevertheless, the command to tear down such strongholds still applies.

As complicated as it is, our brain is an organ subject to dysfunction and disease just like the pancreas, stomach, and all others are. However, remember spiritual strongholds are formed in the mind, and so people who suffer from obsessive-compulsive disorder or other psychological maladies may be more susceptible to their formation, and have more difficulty tearing them down.

The challenges of such dysfunction was the subject of an insightful book from Dr. Ian Osborn, *Can Christianity Cure Obsessive Compulsive Disorder?* In his book, Dr. Osborn examines the life of three great heroes of the faith, Martin Luther, John Bunyan, and Saint Therese—each of whom struggled for years with the assurance of salvation. In his work, Osborn proves beyond reasonable doubt that all three would be competently diagnosed today with OCD.

> In the cases of obsessive-compulsive disorder suffered by Luther, Bunyan and Therese, psychological, cultural, and biochemical factors all played their roles. The obsessions of all three figures began as normal thoughts. Luther, for instance was struck by the common enough concern that he hadn't confessed all his sins. What happened then, however, was something pathological: his mind gave the thought an extra salience that it shouldn't have received...

> From a cultural perspective, Luther, Bunyan, and Therese were all caught up in the epidemic of religious obsessions that began in the early Renaissance... Considering biochemical causes, it seems that Luther, Bunyan, and Therese were all to some extent genetically prone to develop obsessions and compulsions. Most OCD sufferers are. The fact that all three were especially sensitive and guilt-prone when young suggests an inherited predisposition to anxiety.[26]

OCD is characterized by recurrent unwanted thoughts (obsessions) and the repetitive physical or mental behaviors (compulsions) done in attempt to stop the intrusive thoughts and alleviate the emotional distress they cause. To make sense of these of these obsessions, the mind often constructs various narratives that are then acted out in various ways.

For example, in my case as well as for Bunyan, the thought of committing the unpardonable sin became an obsession. Because of the dysfunction within our brain, we could not stop thinking about the possibility of committing such a sin, despite our repulsion of it. Since we could not remove the thoughts from our minds, we developed various mental and physical routines to prove our disdain for it and prevent it from being committed. As a result, the correct understanding and pursuit of the truth of Scripture was supplanted by the all-consuming nature of our obsessions and compulsions regarding the blasphemy of the Holy Spirit. Unbeknownst to us, our efforts to tear down this stronghold, only made it stronger. Thus, one can see the unique way spiritual strongholds can form in individuals with this mental dysfunction and how difficult it can be to tear them down.

The disorder affects roughly 50 million people worldwide; however, that number is probably much higher. Many people with OCD suffer in silence because of stigma, ignorance of the true nature

---

[26] Ian Osborn, *Can Christianity Cure Obsessive Compulsive Disorder* (Grand Rapids; Brazos Press, 2008), 123–24.

of their disorder, or unawareness of effective treatments that are available. Therefore, they never receive an accurate diagnosis or adequate therapy.

That is truly tragic, considering how much we have learned about the disorder in recent years. In fact, current medical research has located three areas of the brain that are implicated in people who suffer from OCD. Maia et al, identifies these three areas and the rationale for their causal role in the development of OCD.

> Three brain areas—the orbitofrontal cortex (OFC), the anterior cingulate cortex (ACC), and the head of the caudate nucleus—have been consistently implicated in a large number of resting, symptom provocation, and pre/post-treatment studies of adults with OCD. These areas (a) are hyperactive at rest in adults with OCD relative to healthy controls, (b) become more active with symptom provocation, and (c) no longer show hyperactivity at rest following successful treatment with either medication or cognitive-behavioral therapy (Baxter, Clark, Iqbal, and Ackermann, 2001; Saxena, Bota, and Brody, 2001; Saxena, Brody, Schwartz, and Baxter, 1998; Saxena and Rauch, 2000; Schwartz, 1998; Whiteside, Port, and Abramowitz, 2004). These findings have generally been interpreted as evidence that abnormalities in these or closely related areas cause OCD (e.g., Baxter et al., 2001; Saxena et al., 2001; Saxena et al., 1998; Saxena and Rauch, 2000).[27]

---

[27] T. V. Maia, R. E. Cooney, B. S. Peterson, "The Neural Bases of Obsessive-Compulsive Disorder in Children and Adults." *Dev Psychopathol*; 20 no. 4 (Fall 2008):1251–83, doi: 10.1017/S0954579408000606. PMID: 18838041; PMCID: PMC3079445.

I mentioned that people who suffer from OCD are more susceptible to spiritual stronghold formations and have greater difficulty in tearing them down. Again, Dr. Schwartz describes physiologically why people who suffer from OCD will have greater difficulty managing their thoughts, emotions, and behaviors.

> Our research on people with OCD at UCLA led us to find that, without question, OCD is a neuropsychiatric illness resulting from a malfunction in the circuitry of the brain... We have good reason to think that the person with OCD can't get rid of those intrusive thoughts and urges because the circuit from the orbital cortex, the brain's "early-warning detection system," is firing inappropriately... Our theory is that since the orbital cortex is modulated by the caudate nucleus, when the caudate nucleus modulation isn't working right, the error detection system in the orbital cortex becomes overactive, and the person has terrible thoughts and feelings that "something is wrong," which leads to compulsive behaviors done in a desperate attempt to make the feelings go away.[28]

The focus of this book is not on mental illness, nor is it assumed that everyone who struggles with assurance has obsessive-compulsive disorder or other psychiatric condition. However, some do, and may not even know it. This makes their effort more difficult, as they must simultaneously overcome their condition while struggling to understand why a settled rest regarding salvation eludes them. More will be said in subsequent chapters on the unique challenges OCD poses in our game plan to gain the assurance of salvation. However, it was appropriate to introduce this topic here alongside our discussion of spiritual strongholds.

---

[28] Ibid., Brain Lock (New York; Harper Collins, 2016), 46, 51, 56.

Hopefully, some clarity was provided regarding the true nature of spiritual strongholds. In their infancy, they are simply thoughts that are diametrically opposed to the truth of God. If such thoughts are not challenged by Scripture, they may become personal opinions, preferences even. In this adolescence stage, if you will, our hearts and actions may evidence only tacit approval of these views. However, before long, such opinions can solidify into beliefs, which are then vigorously defended by our emotions and behaviors. This hostility is the telltale sign of a powerfully mature spiritual stronghold. With this in mind, we will close our discussion of spiritual strongholds with the two common ways Satan and the "old man" forcefully attempt to prevent any incursions into such strategic strongholds.

Dangers of spiritual strongholds: The lion's den and the enchanted ground

The odds of winning a football game, or any sporting event, are always in favor of the home team. This has always been suspected, but a recent analysis across the entire FBS (NCAA Division 1 Football), proved that teams had a 20.3 percent better record at home (62.8 percent) than on the road (42.5 percent) from 2006 to 2016. Therefore, football coaches must make sure their players are prepared for the unique challenges of competing on the opposing team's home field.

The opening chapter quote from Coach "O" describes how difficult it is for visiting opponents to win at LSU's Tiger Stadium. The entire city of Baton Rouge, Louisiana, is abuzz the whole week leading up to a big home game. Tailgates start early and end late, especially when a big rival like Alabama rolls into town. The atmosphere is electric as over a hundred thousand rabid Tiger fans file into that stadium every Saturday. Their cheers are deafening and put fire in the belly of LSU players, while the equally loud boos, taunts, and jeers can steal the heart of the opponent. Coaches do their best to prepare their team to play in such stadiums, but oftentimes that preparation goes out the window when they witness firsthand that type of hostile environment.

In stark contrast, some stadiums appear to offer no real home field advantage. The seats are practically empty, and the few pockets of fans that do show up are scattered throughout the stadium, further diluting any influence they would have on the game. There is no electricity in the air, no excitement, and no anticipation. However, don't be fooled, such stadiums are very dangerous to visiting opponents not used to competing in such an environment. This type of lethargic atmosphere can suck the physical intensity out of players and weaken their mental focus.

As Christians, we are pilgrims in this world and our home field is in heaven. Every one of the battles we face while on earth are "on the road," and as mentioned, battles with spiritual strongholds are in extremely hostile environments!

I described two vastly different types of football stadiums, and the unique challenges each of those home field environments present to the visiting team. I did this to draw parallels to the two types of resistance we will face as we attempt to tear down spiritual strongholds, such as assurance-doubt.

The lion's den

We learned in phase 1 of our game plan, that struggles with assurance is one of Satan's greatest weapons against a believer. He knows that if he is successful, he can establish a formidable stronghold in the mind of the believer. Thus, as Christians get serious about gaining the assurance of salvation, they're often met with spiritual and psychological assaults as they dig deep into their psyche to confront painful emotions and memories. This experience can be extremely intimidating, just like walking into Tiger Stadium!

I call this menacing tactic, the "lion's den" effect. Peter described Satan as a roaring lion, seeking someone to devour (1 Peter 5:8), and many who experience such opposition when first trying to gain victory over a spiritual stronghold, back away in retreat. That said, remember that man always chooses what he perceives benefits him most. Therefore, the existence of a spiritual stronghold—though on the one hand, is a prison we hate—is, on the other hand, a tolerated incarceration.

A spiritual stronghold is tolerated because it meets a deep need and/or deficiency within us. Identifying these personal deficits requires wisdom and grace from the Holy Spirit. Moreover, the Spirit of God must also give us the humility to accept what has been revealed as well as the courage to change any behavior that would keep the stronghold intact (Zechariah 4:6). I will say much more on the perils of the "lion's den" in chapters 8 and 9. Still, for the brave souls who walk through the "lion's den," the danger is just beginning.

The enchanted ground

When Satan realizes his loud roars no longer work, a different tactic is employed. Instead of intimidation, he opts for sedation. If he can't scare you off, he'll lull you to sleep. The process is imperceptible but highly effective, with results better than any anesthesia could elicit. Before long and unbeknownst to you, the urgency, intensity, and focus to make your calling and election sure are mysteriously gone.

I refer to this tactic as the "enchanted ground" effect. For those unfamiliar with Bunyan's classic, Pilgrim's Progress, the enchanted ground was one of the great dangers that Christian and Hopeful faced on their way to the Celestial City. Like playing football in a depressive stadium, the atmosphere of the enchanted ground made any who passed through dull and drowsy.

From personal experience in my quest to gain assurance, I have found the "enchanted ground" much more dangerous than the "lion's den." While in the lion's den, I pressed into the Lord and received much grace, strength, and insight. The experience was painful, but very rewarding.

After winning hard fought battles in the lion's den, I was given rest from the Lord. It's during such periods of peace, that people can wander into the enchanted ground. At least that was true for me, and while there, I became less aware of the obstacles that still needed to be overcome to gain full assurance.

Though I had made great strides in my quest for assurance, the time spent in the enchanted ground necessitated future returns to the lion's den. In chapter 9 I will discuss why return visits to the lion's den often occur and how meditating on specific biblical promises is the key to victory during those times.

Given the danger of the "enchanted ground," it's little wonder that Christians are repeatedly warned in Scripture to be vigilant, sober, and awake. In fact, every author of the New Testament—from Matthew's opening Gospel to John's concluding Apocalypse—includes such warnings. Like the allusions to the synergy of thought, emotion, and action, warnings of the dangers of spiritual lethargy are replete in Scripture.

Final thoughts

These warnings in Scripture are numerous, because Satan and his demonic horde are very real. However, as noted with spiritual strongholds, the general understanding of the spiritual realm, also exists in polar extremes. Too many people today see a demon hiding behind every bush. It's appalling to see TV evangelists casting out "the demon" of everything from diabetes to diarrhea! It's equally distressing to hear liberal theologians dismiss the demonic realm, relegating it alongside goblins, ghouls, and other childish superstitions.

Are spiritual intimidation and delusion as pictured in the "lion's den" and the "enchanted ground," biblically verifiable and dangerous Satanic tactics? Absolutely! However, it must be stressed again that both are only effective against Christians because of the ramifications of the fall. It is the dichotomy that exists within all of us, and the unfortunate dysfunction that exists within some of us, that makes possible the construction and defense of spiritual strongholds. Only with a correct understanding of our culpability regarding spiritual strongholds, are we able to begin the process of tearing them down.

In summary, it's vital to comprehend the spiritual combat we are engaged in as Christians. The malevolent tactics that would rob us of assurance, or any of God's promises are destructive and devious. Spiritual strongholds like assurance-doubt, are built and defended by the "old man" within us and heavily influenced by the demonic realm. Therefore, only the "new man," spurred on by the Spirit of God can tear it down. To do so, however, requires spiritual weapons, which will be the topic of our next chapter.

Mindful question

In the Old Testament, man-made or natural strongholds often became idols. How is the spiritual stronghold of assurance-doubt similar?

5

EQUIPMENT CHECK:
SPIRITUAL ARMOR

As long as we let the Word of God be our only armor,
we can look confidently into the future!
—Dietrich Bonhoeffer

Football is an extremely physical sport. Unfortunately, injuries to players occur often. In attempts to mitigate that danger, a player will wear over twenty separate pieces of equipment. Each piece is specially designed with the latest technology to protect the most vulnerable areas of the body. Also, this protective gear is produced in a variety of sizes to fit each player precisely. This makes properly equipping an entire team very expensive. A football helmet alone can cost $1,000! Multiply that by a hundred-man roster, plus all the other equipment, and any athletic director will confirm that equipping a football team is the most expensive line item on his budget!

Despite the cost, a football player can't compete competently or safely without the proper equipment. Therefore, coaches will conduct regular "equipment checks" to make sure their players' equipment fits properly, is in good condition, and is always being worn.

Similarly, it is folly for us to implement our game plan of tearing down the stronghold of assurance-doubt without first putting on our "spiritual equipment." The battles we face as Christians are more dangerous than any football game, and our opponent is fiercer than any to be met on the gridiron. Thankfully, our equipment, or armor, as Paul describes it, is also specially designed to protect our most vulnerable areas. Moreover, the cost to properly fit each Christian cannot be measured. Our spiritual armor represents six separate line items in the total bill for our redemption, which was purchased by the invaluably precious blood of Christ (Acts 20:28; 1 Corinthians 6:19–20; 1 Peter 1:18–19; Galatians 3:13). The necessity for our spiritual armor and the great price that was paid for its purchase should convince us to regularly put it on. Not to do so, would be foolish and ungrateful.

Only with spiritual armor and weaponry can spiritual strongholds be won. Thus, it is imperative to understand Paul's teaching on this matter. In his epistle to the Ephesians, Paul lists the full armor of God necessary for spiritual battles. In this passage, Paul identifies six specific pieces of spiritual armor. Below is the passage in its entirety.

> Put on the whole armor of God, that you may be able to stand against the schemes of the devil.
>
> For we do not wrestle against flesh and blood, but against the rulers, against the authorities, against the cosmic powers over this present darkness, against the spiritual forces of evil in the heavenly places.
>
> Therefore take up the whole armor of God, that you may be able to withstand in the evil day, and having done all, to stand firm.
>
> Stand therefore, having fastened on the belt of truth, and having put on the breastplate of righteousness,
>
> and, as shoes for your feet, having put on the readiness given by the gospel of peace.
>
> In all circumstances take up the shield of faith, with which you can extinguish all the flaming darts of the evil one;

> and take the helmet of salvation, and the
> sword of the Spirit, which is the word of God,
> praying at all times in the Spirit, with all
> prayer and supplication. (Ephesians 6:12–18a)

It's important to pay close attention to the adjectives Paul uses in this passage and understand his reason for associating those specific words to each piece of armor. For example, Paul purposefully describes the breastplate, as the breastplate of "-righteousness-." He could have referred to it as the breastplate of love, or grace, etc., but he didn't. The same could be said for each piece of armor.

Paul chose his words carefully, under inspiration of the Spirit. Thus, in examining this passage, it is vital to grasp all the insights Paul is conveying in his description of each piece of armor. Not surprisingly, in Paul's description of our spiritual armor we will see again the importance of our thoughts, emotions and actions, along with allusions to their synergy.

1. The belt of truth

Paul begins his list of spiritual armor with the belt of truth. In preparation for battle, a Roman soldier would first bind up the long loose tunic he wore. Once all the slack of his garment was gathered into his crotch, he would wrap it around his waist, tie it in a knot, and secure it with his belt. Only when the belt was firmly in place, could the soldier add the remaining pieces of his armor.

You will recall that Paul told the Corinthians that spiritual strongholds are built upon the thoughts, arguments, and opinions we develop based on the lies we believe. Paul understood the corrupting and metastasizing power of the mind on the whole of man, and therefore begins his armor imagery with the importance of truth.

By truth, the apostle is referring not only to the veracity of Scripture but also the accurate estimation of oneself. Attacks on both have always been a favored tactic of Satan. He successfully plunged humanity into the fall by casting doubt on God's Word (Genesis 3:1), and even had the audacity to tempt Christ with regards to His identity (Matthew 4:6). If Satan tried that tactic on Adam and Jesus, you can be sure he will use it on us!

The great importance of truth is apparent throughout Scripture, but why did Paul associate truth with a soldier's belt? What further insights does the apostle want us to consider? To answer that question, we need to learn about the functions of this critical piece of armor.

A soldier's belt secured not only his tunic but also his breastplate. The belt also had a sheath, which held his sword in place. In short, the belt tied everything together. Similarly, Biblical truth frames our view of reality. Truth binds all our thoughts and experiences into logical coherence. Without truth, man's existence is marked by confusion, meaninglessness, and idolatry. Therefore, Paul charged the Corinthians to take every thought captive that doesn't accord with the truth. Allen picks up on the foundational importance of focusing our thoughts on truth, and his comments will conclude our discussion on this first piece of our spiritual armor.

> Man is made or unmade by himself; in the armory of thought he forges the weapons by which he destroys himself; he also fashions the tools with which he builds for himself heavenly mansions of joy and strength and peace. By the right choice and true application of thought, man ascends to the Divine Perfection, by the abuse and wrong application of thought, he descends below the level of the beast.[29]

2. The breastplate of righteousness

After the soldier's belt has been fastened the next piece of armor to be put on was his breastplate. The breastplate was made of tough material such as leather or brass. It protected the soldier's heart and the organs of the gut.

---

[29] James Allen, *As a Man Thinketh* (New York; Barnes and Nobel, 2007), 4.

In the ancient world, this vital area of the body was seen as the seat of emotions. For the Mesopotamians and the Greeks, the liver was the primary organ where emotions were thought to arise. For the Jews, the heart was commonly associated with emotions (Matthew 12:34; Luke 6:45), but so were the kidneys. Nephrologist, Dr. Joel Kopple, at Harbor-UCLA Medical Center, notes the emotional connection of the kidneys as recorded in the Old Testament.

> In the Bible, the kidneys were considered to be associated with the innermost part of the personality. They were considered central to the soul and to morality. The kidneys were seen as the source or impetus for moral yearning, a force for moral or righteous action and as capable of engendering feelings of guilt or moral approval.[30]

Interestingly, modern medicine has also observed this emotional-visceral connection, referring to the gut as "the second brain" because of the millions of neurons connecting the digestive system with the brain. Writing in Scientific American, Adam Hadhazy interviews Dr. Michael Gershon of Columbia University and UCLA's Dr. Emeran Mayer who affirm the close connection between our brain and gut.

> The second brain informs our state of mind in other more obscure ways, as well. "A big part of our emotions are probably influenced by the nerves in our gut," Mayer says. Butterflies in the stomach-signaling in the gut as part of our physiologic stress response, Gershon says, is but one example. Although gastrointestinal (GI) turmoil can sour one's moods, everyday emotional well-being may rely on messages from the brain

---

[30] Joel D. Kopple, "The Biblical View of the Kidney" (*American Journal of Nephrology*, 14, No. 4–6 (1994), 279–281.

below to the brain above. For example, electrical stimulation of the vagus nerve—a useful treatment for depression-may mimic these signals, Gershon says.[31]

Most theologians agree Paul is connecting the breastplate of righteousness with our emotions. However, this begs two interesting questions. Why does Paul use the term righteousness, and what specific emotions are associated with righteousness?

To answer the first question, Paul is most certainly referring to the imputed righteousness of Christ we receive by faith (Jeremiah 23:6; Romans 3:22, 4:22; 2 Corinthians 5:21). However, he also has in mind practical deeds of righteousness expected to be carried out by all Christians (Romans 12:1; 1 Peter 1:16; 2 Peter 3:11).

In answering the second question, the Scriptures identify the emotion of peace, and the confidence it imparts from both forms of righteousness. The author of Hebrews identifies peace, as the fruit of our practical deeds of righteousness (Hebrews 12:11), and Paul recognizes the peace and confidence we have with God because of our positional righteousness in Christ (Romans 5:1; Eph. 2:14–16).

Before engaging in spiritual battle, we need to be consciously aware of Satan's tactics. In Revelation 12:10, John records hearing a loud voice from heaven identifying Satan as the accuser of the brethren. Day and night, without ceasing, he is pointing the finger at believers. However, he can't lay one single charge against Christ. Therefore, we must be consciously aware that we have the righteousness of Christ.

Our righteous behavior, and the peace it evokes, is a primary means of keeping the reality of our positional righteousness in Christ in the forefront of our minds (Philippians 2:12–13; James 1:23–24; 2 Peter 1:9). After our discussion about the synergy that exists between our thoughts, emotions, and actions, this should not be surprising.

---

[31] Adam Hadhazy, "Think Twice: How the Gut's "Second Brain"—Influences Mood and Well-Being" (*Scientific American;* a division of *Springer Nature*) (February 12, 2010).

Paul further develops both types of righteousness and the resulting emotion of peace with the next item of spiritual armor—shoes fitted with the gospel of peace.

3. Shoes fitted with the Gospel of peace

Paul wastes no time in expressing the importance of our thoughts and emotions by addressing both with the first two pieces of armor; the belt of truth and the breastplate of righteousness. Paul now will speak to the importance of our actions in the tearing down of spiritual strongholds.

Modern views of Western culture differ dramatically at times with that of the Near-Eastern culture of the Bible. Because of that difference, sometimes we miss certain nuances in Scripture. For example, the Jews believed that thoughts, and the emotions they evoked, were not simply hidden and immaterial aspects of one's inmost being. They always manifested in action.

Even the verbal proclamation of the Word was often accompanied by non-verbal demonstrations, and some of those dramatizations must have been quite memorable! For example, the prophecies of the impending doom of the nations of Egypt and Israel were illustrated by Isaiah walking around naked for three years, and Ezekiel cooking his food over excrement.

These vivid enactments continued in the New Testament. Luke records in the book of Acts how Agabus bound himself with Paul's belt to warn of the fate that awaited Paul should he return to Jerusalem. Luke also makes note how Paul symbolically shook off the dust of his garments from the cities that were hostile to him and the Gospel (Acts 21:10–13; 18:6).

Similarly, emotions always manifested themselves in action. Joy was displayed in acts of praise and thanksgiving, while sorrow and regret were publicly portrayed in the wearing of sackcloth and ashes. David dancing before the LORD in jubilant worship (2 Samuel 6:14) and later in humble repentance, clothed in sackcloth and ashes (2 Samuel 6:14; 1 Chronicles 21:16) are prime examples. Tamar described the shameful abuse inflicted upon her as a heavy burden that clung to her (2 Samuel 13:13). Anger sent Abel to his grave, and envy delivered Christ to the cross (Genesis 4:8; Mark 15:10). Every human emotion depicted in the Bible is shown to result in tangible visible actions.

Paul is picturing this importance of action with the imagery of the soldier's shoes. Historians tell us that the shoes of a Roman soldier were often equipped with metal spikes through the soles giving them traction as they advanced through battle. However, the shoes also helped them "dig in" when standing their ground was needed.

I believe this is the primary action Paul has in mind. In fact, Paul tells the Ephesians four separate times before mentioning the shoes, to stand their ground. Paul understood that spiritual assault occurs in our mind and heart. During times of such attack, we must "dig in" and steel our thoughts on truth. As Paul says, "And having done all, to stand firm" (Ephesians 6:13).

To complete this imagery, Paul says our spiritual shoes are not shod with iron spikes, but with the gospel of peace. Obviously, Paul is referring to the good news of the Gospel of Christ. Remember, as we engage spiritual strongholds, we are entering the lion's den. Only by digging our minds deeply into the promises of the Gospel of Christ during spiritual attack, will our peace and confidence be preserved. Listen to the words of Jesus:

> I have said these things to you, that in me you may have peace. In the world you will have tribulation. But take heart; I have overcome the world. (John 16:33)

4. *The shield of faith*

The first three items of our spiritual armor address the centrality of our thoughts, emotions, and actions. The last three items—the shield of faith, helmet of salvation and sword of the Spirit—will do the same. As he discusses these last three pieces of spiritual armor, Paul begins by expressing again the importance of our emotions by introducing the "shield of faith."

The Roman shield, or *skutum*, was roughly two and a half feet wide by four feet in length. It was made of three layers of light, but strong wood glued together and overlaid with leather. In times of battle, Roman soldiers would soak their shields in water to protect against flaming arrows.

The use of flaming arrows was common in the ancient world and were constructed by wrapping fabric around the shaft of the arrow just below the tip. The fabric cloth was then soaked in flammable liquid and ignited. As this construction technique advanced, the shaft of the arrow was filled with incendiary material that would ignite on impact.

Unlike regular arrows, the impact of flaming arrows was not limited to the section of the target it hit. The payload of fire would quickly spread out and engulf much, if not all, of its target. Satan's flaming arrows of temptations are similarly designed. Though their initial target is the emotions and desires of our heart, their damaging effects quickly spreads into our thoughts and actions.

In addition to delivering spreading damage, flaming arrows were also used to scatter and separate Roman soldiers. A main military tactic of Roman soldiers was to form an intricate and impenetrable shield wall called a testudo or tortoise formation. To form the testudo, the first row of soldiers would hold their shields facing forward while the rows behind would overlap their shields over their heads like the tiles of a roof. The formation was so strong that even horses and carts could be driven over it. However, the testudo was only effective if the shields were sufficiently soaked, and if the soldiers were disciplined enough to stay together. Flaming arrows were a weapon of choice to test the integrity of both.

During times of spiritual attack Christians must also band together. As you read through this book, we are banding together through space and time, forming our own testudo, to develop and implement our game plan for tearing down the stronghold of assurance-doubt. Yet it is more important that you seek out other believers to come along side and help you in this area. However, be judicious in the people you choose to form your testudo!

Paul states that our spiritual shield of faith can put out the fiery darts of the evil one, but to be effective our shield must be soaked with the water of the Word of God (Romans 10:17; Ephesians 5:26). Therefore, do not seek counsel from Christians who are neither wise nor skilled in the Scriptures, lest your struggles with the assurance worsen. With that in mind, we now turn our attention to the next piece of armor, the helmet of salvation.

5.   The helmet of salvation

Of all the pieces of armor Paul describes, the helmet of salvation is perhaps the most crucial for those struggling with assurance. For that reason, we will need to spend more time to adequately develop this piece of spiritual armor.

Commonly, Roman helmets were made of tough thick leather covered with bands of metal plates. However, some were made entirely of molded metal with leather on the inside for padding. All Roman soldiers were issued a helmet and were required to wear it during battle to protect against crippling or lethal blows to the head. Therefore, the Roman soldier guarded and treasured his helmet, and would often inscribe his name inside of it.

You will recall that Paul began his list of armor with the belt of truth—the truth of Scripture; and the truth regarding our identity as Christians. These are the key truths our minds must focus on during spiritual combat related to assurance. To harness that focus, Paul says we are to put on the helmet of salvation. It is obvious that Paul is drawing our attention to the importance of the mind with this piece of armor, but why does he call it the helmet of salvation? To answer that question, we need to understand Satan's tactics.

Paul understood that a favorite strategy of Satan is to get a believer to doubt each aspect of his salvation. That is why he calls our spiritual helmet, "the helmet of salvation." Satan knows it's impossible to prevent our salvation, but he also knows it's highly possible to convince us that it can be. Thus, it is vital for us to be aware of Satan's game plan in this regard. That's right, Satan has a game plan too, and included in it is a scouting report on each one of us!

With that in mind, I noted the importance coaches place on developing thorough scouting reports on both their opponents, as well as their own players (self-scouts). To illustrate the profound impact such information can have on a team, I will share an interesting account a friend of mine had when he was a college football player.

My friend's coaches somehow got a copy of the opposing team's scouting report. A special meeting was called, and the report was shared with the entire team. At first, my friend thought that it was a self-scout report done by his own coaches that was being read, because of the personal nature of the information. However, as the head coach continued reading, it became apparent that the report came from their upcoming opponent. It's one thing to hear critiques from your own coach, but quite another when your flaws are pointed out by the opposing staff!

He told me it was infuriating to hear their personal weaknesses exposed by the opposing coaches! Now, whether this report was truly obtained from another team or was simply a unique and impactful way of delivering a self-scouting report by his own coaches, my friend cannot say. However, he did say that particular scouting report made his team more focused and determined than ever before. Hearing the truth hurt, but it made them better!

The reason for sharing my friend's story is to make you more determined and focused than ever to gain the assurance of your salvation. Our opponent, Satan, has certainly scouted us and has put that report in his game plan. He knows the key areas to attack are each aspect of our salvation. He also knows our personal weaknesses. Thus, it behooves us to do a "self-scout" to assess our own understanding of salvation, and to predict the ways Satan will entice us to doubt.

Since the experience worked so well for my friend, for the following section it might be helpful to imagine you are in the "Team Room," receiving your *Salvation Scouting Report* for the first time. I will be your head coach and will begin by giving you a breakdown of the significance of each aspect of your salvation. These are your top four areas of strength, and your understanding and belief in them is where your opponent is likely to strike.

Thus, once you understand each aspect of your salvation, I will discuss the anticipated strategies that will be used against you, and how the helmet of salvation will be your key armor of defense. So grab a seat in the Team Room, and let the following report make you more determined than ever to gain the assurance of your salvation!

In chronological order, the first aspect of our salvation is Declaration. You may have heard this referred to as the Doctrine of Election. Our salvation was declared by God Himself in eternity past (Matthew 25:32–34; Ephesians 1:4) Before we were even born or done anything good or bad (Romans 9:11–13), God sovereignly declared that all Christians will be saved.

This second aspect of our salvation is called Justification. It refers to the specific time in our life that we came to faith in Christ. Justification happens only once and it is an immediate and irrevocable imputation of Christ's righteousness to the believer (Romans 4:4–5, 5:18–19; 2 Corinthians 5:21).

The third aspect of our salvation is called Sanctification, which is the work of the Holy Spirit to conform us into Christlikeness (1 Corinthians 1:2, 6:11;2 Thessalonians 2:13; Hebrews 10:14). Unlike justification, sanctification is a continuous process that we participate in, and lasts until we die.

The fourth and final aspect of our salvation is called Glorification. This refers to our ultimate delivery from sin and death via the provision of our new resurrected bodies. In the glorified state, we will live in the new heaven and earth with God forever (John 14:1–3;1 John 3:2; Philippians 3:20–21; Hebrews 11:16).

These four aspects of our salvation are guaranteed by God; therefore, they are the key areas that will be attacked by Satan. Satan knows he cannot stop God from fulfilling His promises, but he knows he can get you to doubt them. What follows, are some of Satan's favorite strategies to cast doubt on each aspect of your salvation.

Attacks on declaration

St. Augustine said, "We were not chosen because we chose Christ. We chose Christ because we were chosen." The doctrine of election, or declaration as I have referred to it, is the most difficult aspect of our salvation to comprehend. At first glance, it appears to make God arbitrary, capricious even.

We perceive election this way for two main reasons. First, because we have very little appreciation for just how wicked man is, and how holy and gracious God is. The second reason is, we simply have not thought through the matter logically. After all, even people who don't believe in election still have to wrestle with the question; "why would an all-powerful and loving God not save everyone?" Dr. Tim Keller is much smarter than me, so I'll let him answer that question.

> So why doesn't he? We can only know two things. First, the answer must have something to do with his perfect nature. He is perfectly loving and perfectly righteous, and neither can be preferred over the other or he wouldn't be God. Somehow the answer has to do with his being consistent with himself. Second, we cannot see the whole picture. Why? If we can conceive of a more merciful system of salvation than God has, we must not see it rightly, for God is more merciful than we can ever imagine. Indeed, when we finally see the whole plan and answer, we will not be able to find fault with it.[32]

Nevertheless, as difficult as this aspect of our salvation is to grasp, it is clearly taught in Scriptures (John 6:44, 15:16–17; Romans 8:29–30; Ephesians 1:4; 2 Thessalonians 2:13; 2 Timothy 1:9). As

---

[32] Tim Keller, *3 Objections to the Doctrine of Election*; (The Gospel Coalition, INC., 2023), September 21, 2015.

I will demonstrate in chapter 9, a correct understanding of the doctrine of election is very helpful to gain the assurance of salvation. Therefore, we can expect Satanic attack upon it.

Satan will cast doubt on the aspect of declaration by calling into question God's sovereignty and fairness. He will do anything to distract you from working out your own salvation and making your calling and election sure (Philippians 2:12; 2 Peter 1:10). If he senses you are getting closer to that end he hisses objections, "What about the person who never heard the Gospel?" "God is not fair—He can't be trusted." When such temptations are no longer effective, he'll use what worked on Bunyan and countless others, that is, he will get you to doubt your own election. Remember the opening quote taken from *Grace Abounding*?

"I began to find my soul to be assaulted with fresh doubts… How can you tell you are elected? And what if you should not?… By these things I was driven to my wits' end."

Bunyan is not alone in suffering such an attack on his election. Even the great Baptist preacher, Charles Spurgeon admitted he endured such assaults.

> "I must confess here, with sorrow, that I have seasons of despondency and depression of spirit, which I trust none of you are called to suffer, and at such times I have doubted my interest in Christ, my calling, my election, my perseverance, my Savior's blood, and my Father's love."[33]

The doctrine of election is chronologically the first aspect of our salvation. Despite our difficulty to comprehend it, it is every bit as true, gracious, and trustworthy as the following three we will discuss. If Satan attacks giants of the faith like Bunyan and Spurgeon in this regard, none of us are safe! I can attest, that understanding this doctrine was the final key for making my own calling and election sure.

---

[33] Charles Spurgeon, "The Glorious Right Hand of the Lord," (*The Charles Spurgeon Sermon Collection*, ed. Emmett O'Donnell), (2023).

Attacks on justification

Satan assaults justification by inciting believers to doubt the manner, motivations, and sincerity in which they came to faith in Christ. Few people come to Christ in spectacular ways as did Paul or Luther. Some people were saved amid debilitating sin, while others were spared such heartbreak. The former can often point to the exact day and circumstances surrounding their conversion, while the latter may not recall how or when they came to Christ.

Some people may have been saved in a small country church, while others at a packed stadium during a Billy Graham revival. Satan wants you to doubt your salvation by contrasting it with someone else's conversion experience. However, Paul said it is not wise to compare ourselves among ourselves (2 Corinthians 10:12). In fact, Paul says it's a symptom of carnality and worldliness when we make comparisons of how and by whom we came to faith.

> For ye are yet carnal: for whereas there is among you envying, and strife, and divisions, are ye not carnal, and walk as men? For while one saith, I am of Paul; and another, I am of Apollos; are ye not carnal? Who then is Paul, and who is Apollos, but ministers by whom ye believed, even as the Lord gave to every man? (1 Corinthians 3:3–5 KJV)

Satan will also tempt you to doubt your salvation by casting aspersions on your motivations for becoming a Christian. He accusatively whispers that you came to Christ solely, "to get out of the mess you made," "so your spouse would marry you," "to avoid going to hell," etc.

We are all unique individuals, with our own faults, fears, and struggles. However, what's common to all Christians is the recognition of our inability to save ourselves. When each person comes to Christ, they do so because they believe that only He can save them. Yet it's impossible as human beings not to have a variety of motivations present within us, even at the time of conversion. To illustrate this, let's look at an interesting account in the life of David that demonstrates this tension.

To set the context, King Saul and all of Israel were at war with the Philistines. The battle lines were drawn, and it was only a matter of time before a full-scale confrontation occurred. So David's father sent him down with provisions for his brothers who were soldiers stationed at the front line.

When he arrived, David heard Goliath challenging the armies of Israel and defying the God of heaven. David was filled with zeal for God's glory and was outraged by the words of Goliath. However, the Bible also states that David asked on two separate occasions what reward would there be for the man who would kill this Philistine (1 Samuel 17:25–30). Each time David asked, the soldiers answered that, King Saul offered riches, the hand of his daughter in marriage, and freedom for the man's family who would slay the giant.

Nobody would say that David only went out against the giant Goliath to marry Saul's daughter, or to gain riches. David's main motivation was the honor of God. Yet David was also interested in Saul's reward. The same is true of us at the time of justification. Our pressing need is to be delivered from our helplessness to save ourselves, yet we can't deny the desire for the great riches of Christ in heaven. Even Peter asked Jesus what reward would be for himself and the other disciples for following Him (Matthew 19:27).

The same logic can be applied for our dreading of hell. As Spurgeon said, "We rob the Gospel of its power if we leave out it's threatenings of punishment." In fact, I will use my own testimony to illustrate the wisdom of Spurgeon's assertion.

My football coach in college led me to the Lord. During that conversation he explained the Gospel to me, and when he finished, he quoted two Scriptures, "that today was the day of salvation" (2 Corinthians 6:2) and that "the Spirit of God will not always strive with man" (Genesis 6:3).

Through my coach's words, the Holy Spirit first opened my eyes to see my need of Christ, and then warned me of the danger of not responding accordingly. Those warnings were necessary and effective. For as I was under conviction, Satan (and the "old man" within) was tempting me with thoughts such as, "What will your parents and friends think?" "You will change into one of those "Holy-Rollers," and many other fearful thoughts.

However, Isaiah says we are to sanctify the LORD of hosts Himself; and let Him be your fear and let Him be your dread (Isaiah 8:13). Jesus issued this warning, "But I will warn you whom to fear: fear him who, after he has killed, has authority to cast into hell. Yes, I tell you, fear him!" (Luke 12:5). In the book of Revelation, John alludes to the causal role fear can have in preventing one from coming to Christ.

> But the fearful, and unbelieving, and the abominable, and murderers, and whoremongers, and sorcerers, and idolaters, and all liars, shall have their part in the lake which burneth with fire and brimstone: which is the second death. (Revelation 21:8 KJV)

I believed the Bible and understood my need of Christ, but I was also being assaulted by fearful thoughts. The warnings of Scripture my coach shared, melted those fears like wax before the greater fear of God.

Finally, Satan will attack your sincerity at conversion. As is the case with manner and motivation, it is unwise to look for a universal standard with regards to sincerity. Some people simply feel things more intensely than others. Upbringing, life experiences, along with the way God made us—all influence how passionately we process emotions. Not only is sincerity not similar for all, but sincerity is not always in a steady state. It has been my experience that the longer I have been a Christian the more aware I have become of my own sinfulness, and more appreciative of my salvation.

When the great Puritan preacher, John Owen was asked how much conviction was necessary for a person to feel when coming to Christ, he wisely answered, "just enough for them to come to Christ"!

Attacks on sanctification

The third aspect of our salvation is sanctification, and like the first two (declaration and justification) we discussed, expect Satanic assaults. Again, the enemy knows he can do nothing to prevent any of the four aspects of your salvation from occurring, but he can derail your trust and faith in them.

I stated earlier that the aspect of sanctification is unique as it occurs jointly between us and the Holy Spirit. Take a wild guess who falters in holding up their end of the bargain! It is precisely those areas of neglect in our Christian walk that Satan will constantly bring up to cause you to doubt your salvation. We will fully develop this phenomenon in chapter 7, but it's necessary to briefly mention three important considerations of our sanctification now. To guide our discussion, we will look at a familiar verse from the book of Psalms listed below.

> And he shall be like a tree planted by the rivers of water, that bringeth forth his fruit in his season; his leaf also shall not wither; and whatsoever he doeth shall prosper. (Psalm 1:3 KJV)

In this first chapter, the psalmist contrasts the righteous and the wicked man. The righteous man is being pictured as a tree planted by rivers of water. We have already discussed that we received the righteousness of Christ at our conversion (justification). The "rivers of water" is a clear reference to the sanctifying work of the Holy Spirit in the life of a Christian, as Jesus affirms in John's Gospel.

> On the last day of the feast, the great day, Jesus stood up and cried out, "If anyone thirsts, let him come to me and drink.
> Whoever believes in me, as the Scripture has said, 'Out of his heart will flow rivers of living water.'"

Now this he said about the Spirit, whom
those who believed in him were to receive, for as
yet the Spirit had not been given, because Jesus
was not yet glorified. (John 7:37–39)

As I mentioned, there are three important facets of your sanctification pictured in this verse. Specifically, that your sanctification
is promised, personal, and progressive. Understanding each of these
three features is critical in our game plan to gain the assurance of
salvation and therefore require a closer look at this passage from the
Psalter.

First, notice that the verse begins with, *"And he shall be..."* and
ends with, *"his leaf shall not wither."* Here, the psalmist is assuring us
that our sanctification will happen. It is a promise of God, and Satan
knows he cannot stop its inevitability. Below are just a few verses
proving the certainty of our sanctification.

For by a single offering he has perfected for
all time those who are being sanctified. (Hebrews
10:14)

So Jesus also suffered outside the gate in
order to sanctify the people through his own
blood. (Hebrews 13:12)

And because of him you are in Christ Jesus,
who became to us wisdom from God, righteousness and sanctification and redemption. (1
Corinthians 1:30)

Just as we have borne the image of the man
of dust, we shall also bear the image of the man
of heaven. (1 Corinthians15:49)

Our sanctification is not only promised but it is also personal.
The psalmist says that the righteous will bring forth *"his fruit."* Again,

Satan always wants you to doubt your salvation, and his favorite tactic is to get you to compare yourself with others. Remember, Paul said that was a foolish thing to do (2 Corinthians 10:12).

We have all been given different gifts according to the grace given to us, and we have all been given different measures of faith in which to exercise those gifts (Romans 12:3–6). Your gifts and talents were specially picked for you to help you complete your specific assignments in the Kingdom (Romans 12:4–6a; 1 Corinthians 12:4–5; 1 Peter 4:10). Christ illustrated this in his "Parable of the Talents" (Matthew 25:14–30).

The LORD has different assignments, which require different gifts for each of us. To counter Satan's tactics, we must not only trust that Christ will ensure our eventual sanctification, but we must also graciously and gratefully accept the way He chooses to do it. Of course, the primary way our sanctification is achieved is through the diligent study of His Word. So the psalmist says the righteous man meditates day and night on the Word (Psalms 1:2). In Christ's High Priestly prayer, He confirms the same.

> Sanctify them through thy truth: thy word
> is truth. (John 17:17 KJV)

Finally, in addition to being promised and personal, our sanctification is progressive. We already mentioned that we do not become sinless at conversion. The "old man" won't go away until our time on this earth is done. Therefore, the psalmist says that the righteous will bring for his fruit in, "*his season.*"

Here again we must be aware of Satan's propensity to accuse you when you don't measure up to somebody else's progress in the faith. All Christians will produce fruit but not all at the same time. God is the vine dresser (John 15:1–2) and He will prune us at the appropriate time for our fruit to come in our season. When our season does come, God will not only ensure a bountiful crop but hasten its harvest.

The least one shall become a clan, and the
smallest one a mighty nation; I am the LORD; in
its time I will hasten it (Isaiah 60:22).

Attacks on glorification

The final aspect of our salvation is Glorification. Like the first three, it is a promise of God that no power in the universe can stop (Romans 8:38). Unfortunately, also like the first three, it is easy for us to doubt. In fact, Glorification may be the easiest aspect of our salvation to doubt.

We mentioned that sanctification was the only aspect of our salvation that was a collaborative effort. Though we do not work jointly with God to enter the glorified state, it nonetheless requires us to experience two separate events that are very scary for us. We need to die, and we need to leave this earth.

Fear of dying is universal to the human race (Hebrews 2:15). The physical pain normally experienced at death plays a big part in that fear, as does the emotional pain of grief and loneliness. Even though, we know our ultimate destination as Christians is far better than experienced here, we fear the transition.

Fear is a powerful emotion that can very easily and quickly cause us to doubt. None of the first three aspects of our salvation, require us to face the full weight of fear like glorification does. Therefore, none of the first three aspects of our salvation will produce as many doubts. We will develop the relationship of fear and doubt further in chapter 8, but it is important to stress here.

However, fear of physical and emotional pain are not the only hurdles to overcome at glorification. We not only have to experience death, but we also must undergo the biggest change we have ever faced.

Any change is scary, even good ones. As fallen creatures, we tend to hold on tightly to what's familiar. This can be seen in people who have been incarcerated for many years. Upon release, they often commit another crime, solely to return to the familiar confines of the prison walls. The fall has hindered our ability to trust as well.

This explains our insatiable need to be in total control of our circumstances, environment, and destination. On our death beds we have no more control and must do what comes very hard for us. We must trust.

In chapter 9, we will discuss the reasons why we doubt our eventual glorification, and how meditating on specific scriptures will increase our trust. Until then, rest in these most comforting words of Christ.

> Let not your hearts be troubled. Believe in God; believe also in me.
>
> In my Father's house are many rooms. If it were not so, would I have told you that I go to prepare a place for you?
>
> And if I go and prepare a place for you, I will come again and will take you to myself, that where I am you may be also. (John 14:1–3)

To close our discussion on the helmet of salvation, I have two final thoughts. First, it was mentioned that each Roman soldier was issued a helmet and was required to wear it in times of battle. We too have been issued a helmet, not by some Roman bureaucrat, but by God Himself, and He commands us to put it on by faith. As you put your helmet on, remember the four aspects of your salvation are promised, and nothing can prevent any of God's promises from being fulfilled.

Paul confirms the inevitability of each aspect of our salvation in what is often called the Golden Chain of Redemption. I highly recommend you memorize this marvelous passage of Scripture!

> For those whom he foreknew he also predestined to be conformed to the image of his Son, in order that he might be the firstborn among many brothers.
>
> And those whom he predestined he also called, and those whom he called he also justi-

fied, and those whom he justified he also glorified. (Romans 8:28–30)

Lastly, I noted that it was common practice for a soldier
to inscribe his name inside his helmet. We are a new creation (2
Corinthians 5:17) and we have a new name that will be given to us
by Christ (Revelation 2:17). Our new name reflects our new identity
as believers. Though we do not know what our new name will be,
we inscribe our faith inside our helmet of salvation by holding on
to the truth of Scriptures, and the truth of who we are in Christ.
Remember, the evil one will certainly tempt us in both areas.

Hopefully, imagining being in the Team Room and hearing the
common strategies Satan uses to rob believers of their assurance by
attacking the four aspects of salvation has helped. Like my friend and
his teammates, allow this scouting report to light a fire in you, and
keep it burning until you have won your assurance!

6. The Sword of the Spirit

The first five pieces of armor we discussed were all defensive
in nature. Paul closes his list of spiritual armor with a very powerful
offensive weapon, the sword of the Spirit. Just as Paul commanded us
to "take up" the whole armor of God, he likewise commands us to;
"take up the sword of the Spirit," which is the Word of God. In keeping with our football theme, Paul is telling us to get off the sidelines;
and get into the game and fight!

A Roman sword was called a gladius. It was a very sharp, dou-
ble-edged sword. It was roughly two feet long, ideally crafted for
close hand-to-hand combat. The author of Hebrews describes the
Word of God similarly.

For the word of God is living and active,
sharper than any two-edged sword, piercing to
the division of soul and of spirit, of joints and of
marrow, and discerning the thoughts and intentions of the heart. (Hebrews 4:12)

Though the gladius was expertly designed, it was only deadly on the battlefield in the hand of a highly trained soldier. Therefore, all Roman soldiers went through a very intense boot camp lasting four months. During, this time they were taught how to wield their sword efficiently. As Christians we also need to be trained in the Word, to wield it properly.

> Do your best to present yourself to God as one approved, a worker who has no need to be ashamed, rightly handling the word of truth (2 Timothy 2:15).

The Roman soldier's training in swordsmanship continued after boot camp, with daily sparring bouts with fellow soldiers, not to mention live battles with enemies. Indeed, their training never ended, but only got more advanced. This recognition for the need of continual advanced training is the same mindset we are to have with our spiritual sword, the Word of God. Again, the author of Hebrews affirms this.

> In fact, though by this time you ought to be teachers, you need someone to teach you the elementary truths of God's word all over again. You need milk, not solid food!
> Anyone who lives on milk, being still an infant, is not acquainted with the teaching about righteousness.
> But solid food is for the mature, who by constant use have trained themselves to distinguish good from evil. (Hebrews 5:12–14)

The author of Hebrews laments the immature faith of his audience and explains that it is due to their ignorance of the Word of God. They remain ignorant simply because they refused to consistently apply it to their life.

Being ignorant of, or negligent in the use of the Word of God has consequences. Hosea says, "My people are destroyed for lack of knowledge" (Hosea 4:6a). The dangers we face when tearing down spiritual strongholds are very real and extremely powerful. We certainly need our defensive armor, but to gain ground we need to be on the attack. We not only need to study the Word of God, but to become truly skilled in wielding the sword of the Spirit, we must get into the fight and use it!

In closing, I will discuss one more rigorous aspect of training the Roman soldiers endured, "the march." The first thing the Roman soldiers were taught to do was to march. Early on in their training, they were taught how to march in unison. Once they mastered that, they were taught how to deploy swiftly and orderly into a variety of different battle formations. Marching was the foundational component of the training regimen of the Roman army, with daily marches of twenty miles or more.

The goal for these marches however was not just to increase conditioning or to execute military tactics. The march taught the Roman soldiers the importance of collaboration, cohesion, and obeying commands.

No doubt the apostle Paul, had seen hundreds of skillfully synchronized Roman marches. It's possible that images of those marches crossed his mind as he closes his discourse on spiritual armor with the command to pray in the Spirit. However, if that is true, we need we need to examine what praying in the Spirit means.

To understand all that is entailed in praying in the Spirit, first consider that Paul describes our spiritual armor as the "armor of God," and our weapon as the "sword of the Spirit." So really it is not our armor or our weapon, but God's. Thus, as we put on our spiritual armor and take up our spiritual weapon, we fall under His authority. Moreover, in wearing God's armor we become in tune with God, and our prayers reflect that unity. Not only unity with God, but also with our fellow soldiers in the faith. Therefore, Paul says to make supplications for all the saints (Ephesians 6:18). John Piper is very helpful in explaining what it means to pray in the Spirit.

> Here's my suggestion for what "praying in the Spirit" means: it means that our prayers are moved and guided by the Holy Spirit. That is, we are being prompted to pray by the Spirit; He's awakening it and moving it. And the things that we pray for are being shaped and determined by the Spirit. So it's His power that carries the prayer, and it's His leading that guides the prayer.[34]

Like a Roman centurion—who organizes, commands, and employs his soldiers effectively in their march objectives—the Holy Spirit also determines and directs our prayers in the battles we face. In addition, since the Holy Spirit is the driving force behind our prayers, it is by his authority that our prayers are obeyed in the spiritual realm. Visualizing yourself as a Roman soldier, clad in spiritual armor, marching in unison with your fellow soldiers under the commands and authority of the Holy Spirit, is a powerful image to meditate on as you enter into Spirit led prayer amid the spiritual battles of your life.

This concludes our discussion of spiritual armor. As mentioned at the beginning of this chapter, the synergy of our thoughts, emotions and actions was evident in each piece of our spiritual armor. The belt of truth and helmet of salvation secure our mind in truth and protect against the lies of the devil by focusing our thoughts on the promises of God. To protect our emotions from being ignited by the fiery darts of the evil one, we also have two pieces of specialized armor; the shield of faith and the breastplate of righteousness. Finally, we put on our spiritual shoes and take up the sword of the Spirit when standing our ground or advancing into the hostile terri-

---

[34] John Piper, How Do We Pray in the Spirit?" (Desiring God Foundation, desiringGod.org), August 2, 2021.

tory of spiritual strongholds is required. Both are obvious allusions to the importance of our actions.

As you put on your spiritual armor by faith, remember the central importance of your mind, heart, and behavior and how they synergistically influence each other for good or ill. To help visualize this relationship I added our spiritual armor into the TEA graph and chart below.

SPIRITUAL   ARMOR

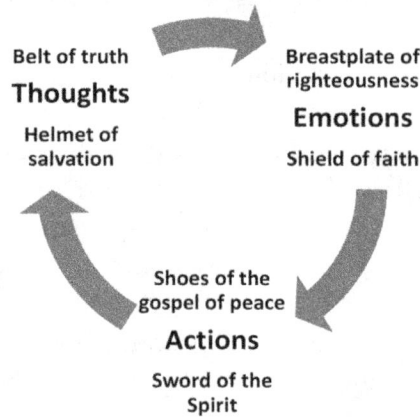

Thoughts	Emotions	Actions
Belt of truth	Breastplate of righteousness	Shoes of the gospel of peace
Helmet of salvation	Shield of faith	Sword of the Spirit

Finally, to gain the assurance of our salvation we must be determined and equipped to do so. Assurance-doubt is a powerful spiritual stronghold erected by Satan and the "old man." Only the "new man," clad in spiritual armor, and in the power of the Holy Spirit, can tear such a fortress down.

We have covered a lot of material thus far in our game plan. Therefore, before we identify and begin discussion of the *five obsta-*

cles to the assurance of salvation a brief review is necessary. However, please complete your mindful question before beginning the review in the next chapter.

Mindful question

During our discussion of the helmet of salvation, we stated that Satan causes us to doubt our salvation by enticing us to compare ourselves with other believers. Describe the specific circumstances when you fallen into this trap.

6

MONDAY WALK-THROUGH:
FIRST REVIEW

Not by might, nor by power, but by my
Spirit, says the LORD of hosts.
—Zechariah, the prophet

Football coaches have their game plans finished by late Sunday night. Many hours of film study and analysis have been logged in its completion. All the information gathered on the upcoming opponent as well as the data logged from the self-scouts are then condensed into a few clear objectives to be implemented in the upcoming week of practice. The implementation and mastery of these major objectives comprises phase 4 of a game plan.

Before heading out to the field for practice on Monday, the game plan objectives are explained one by one with the players in the Team Room. These key objectives are then demonstrated on the practice field in a very slow and highly structured pace. Coaches call this formal review of the game plan objectives, the "Monday walk-through."

Thus far we have been structuring our game plan for assurance in the same way a football game plan is. Now it's time to do our "Monday walk-through," where we review the critical information

incorporated into our game plan and identify our key objectives—
the *five obstacles to the assurance of salvation.*

Where we've been: Phases 1–3

To begin our review, it has been demonstrated that struggles
with assurance has been a common and significant problem for
believers, past and present. It is a problem that has serious consequences for the individual believer as well as for the entire body of
Christ. Therefore, the Bible commands us to make our calling and
election sure (2 Peter 1:10).

We have determined that the impediments to assurance can
be broadly, yet definitively, associated with a person's thoughts,
emotions, and actions. The close synergistic relationship that exists
between these three, has been demonstrated both scripturally and by
current medical and psychological research. Therefore, any destructive and unchallenged thought, emotion, or behavior will eventually
have a negative impact on the other two.

This underlying negative synergism between a person's thoughts,
emotions, and actions is the root cause for severe and prolonged
struggles with assurance and explains why the Westminster divines
affirmed that to attain assurance a believer, *"may wait long, and conflict with many difficulties, before he be partaker of it."*[35] The Bible
says, "The cord of three strands is not easily broken" (Ecclesiastes
4:12), and that is certainly true with regards to the negative synergy
between our thoughts, emotions, and actions!

We have also seen that struggles with assurance have a very real
spiritual component as well. Indeed, assurance-doubt is a strategic
spiritual stronghold the enemy seeks to establish and maintain in
the life of a believer. To our horror, we realized that the old earthly
man within us; is complicit in forming and defending spiritual
strongholds. Thus, only the new spiritual man, clad with spiritual
armor, and empowered by the Holy Spirit, can tear down spiritual
strongholds.

---

[35] Ibid., WCF Section III.

Where we're going: Phase 4

Now that our review is complete, it is time to distill our game plan down to our key objectives. The remainder of this book will focus specifically on the five major obstacles to the assurance of salvation. As with the previous chapters, each obstacle will be discussed from a scriptural and scientific perspective.

Introducing the five obstacles to the assurance of salvation

What follows are the five obstacles we must overcome to gain the assurance of our salvation. I have placed them in our TEA graph to depict how their synergistic relationship leads to the spiritual stronghold of assurance-doubt.

As we discuss each obstacle, it is critical to remember that the initial impetus that starts the negative cycle of synergy is irrelevant, as the result is the same. For example, the obstacle *uncommitted in walk* placed under our actions, will inevitably affect the other obstacles located within the TEA graph and lead to the spiritual stronghold of assurance-doubt if it is not overcome.

Five obstacles to the assurance of salvation

1. Unbiblical in Foundation
2. Undisciplined in Mind
3. Unrestored in Emotions
4. Uncommitted in Walk
5. *Unsaved in Reality

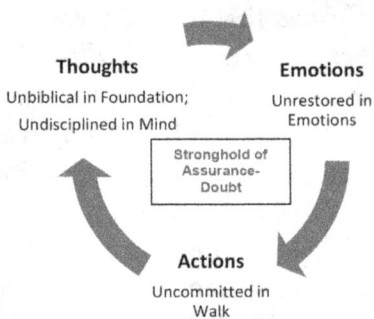

At this point you will notice that one of the five obstacles, *unsaved in reality*, is not located within the TEA graph and is offset by itself. Before I explain the reason for that, we need to understand the four different types of people and their unique perspectives concerning the assurance of salvation. R. C. Sproul identifies these four categories of people.

1. Those who are saved and know they are.
2. Those who are saved but don't think they are.
3. Those who are unsaved and know they aren't.
4. Those who are unsaved but think they are.

The first four obstacles to be discussed will be applicable to the spiritual stronghold of assurance-doubt. Thus, these obstacles will be specific to the first two categories of people described by Sproul; those who have genuine saving faith, whether conscious of it or not.

As the title suggests, the main objective of this book is to help genuine believers who wrestle with doubts concerning their salvation (Sproul's second category). The first four obstacles located within the TEA graph are specific obstacles that these genuine believers must overcome to gain assurance.

For those Christians who have no doubts as to their salvation (Sproul's first category), this book will primarily serve as a resource to understand and help counsel those who do struggle, and to protect against future struggles with assurance of their own.

The last obstacle, *unsaved in reality*, is most applicable for those not yet in a state of grace, whether they know it or not. These are the last two categories of people Sproul describes. However, the ramifications of this obstacle make it relevant to all. Thus, the Scriptural charge for self-examination (2 Corinthians 13:5).

Moreover, the obstacle *unsaved in reality* is associated with an entirely separate spiritual stronghold that we will discuss thoroughly in the chapter 10. Please complete this review by finishing the "Mindful Question."

Mindful question

Before continuing on to the remaining chapters, fill out your Self-scout report by identifying the key topics or ideas that resonated most with your individual struggle for assurance.

Game Plan for the Assurance of Salvation

Game Plan Phase	Key Concepts	Self-Scout (Record one or two ideas from each phase of our game plan that had the most impact for you personally.)
Chapter 1 Phase 1: Gathering general/ contextual information.	1. Personal history 2. Prevalence of the problem 3. Priority of pursuit 4. Primacy of the problem	
Chapter 2 Phase 2: Player identification.	1. Thoughts 2. Emotions 3. Actions	
Chapter 3 Phase 3: Schemes and Tendencies.	1. Scheme: Synergy 2. Tendency: Negative	
Chapter 4 The Venue	Spiritual stronghold	
Chapter 5 Equipment Check	Spiritual armor	
Chapter 6 Monday Walkthrough	Review and identify key objectives	
Chapters 7–11 Phase 4: Implementation of key objectives.	1. Unbiblical in Foundation 2. Undisciplined in Mind 3. Unrestored in Emotions 4. Uncommitted in Walk 5. Unsaved in Reality	Leave this blank until you have completed the book.

7

GAME PLAN—PHASE 4:
IMPLEMENTATION

UNCOMMITTED IN WALK

Change your conduct or change your name!
—Alexander the Great

Importance of implementation

Tuesday, April 23, 1985—lovers of Coca-Cola call it Black Tuesday. It was the ill-fated day for the launch of New Coke. After decades of dominance, Coke was engaged in a fierce battle with Pepsi during the so-called "cola wars" of the 1980s. The Pepsi Challenge, a taste-test ad campaign, reporting most Americans preferred the sweet taste of Pepsi over Coke was a huge success. As a result, Pepsi had finally replaced Coke as the number one cola in the US.

In response to their hemorrhaging market share, Coca-Cola executives decided to scrap the original hundred-year-old formula of Coke for the much sweeter version of New Coke. Although the strategy made some sense, the implementation could not have gone worse. In fact, it was an unmitigated disaster, costing Coca-Cola millions of dollars in lost revenue. Within a few months, "Original Coke" was back on the shelves, while New Coke became "exhibit A" for botched implementation strategies in MBA programs across the country!

The example of Coca-Cola reinforces the reality that regardless of how much time, thought and effort has gone into developing your key objectives, if you don't implement them properly, they're useless, even a liability. Emphasizing the importance of implementation, Jamie Dimon, CEO of JPMorgan Chase, said, "I'd rather have a first-rate execution and second-rate strategy any time, rather than a brilliant idea and mediocre management."

I could not agree more with Dimon. In my experience in coaching and in business, I have seen very good plans fail because of poor implementation. In fact, failing to execute on organizational strategy in the business world is woefully common, with 90 percent of corporations falling short of successfully implementing their key objectives.[36] Apparently, the lessons from New Coke continue to fall on deaf ears.

There are many reasons business plans fall apart at this critical stage, while football game plans tend not to. The reasons for failure are many, but my top three should be sufficient to prove my case.

The first reason for failure is that in the business world, the key objectives of the plan are often poorly defined. Plan objectives must be clear and easy to comprehend. A major reason corporations are unsuccessful in implementing their key objectives is because 95 percent of employees do not know or understand their organization's strategy.[37] Not so with a football game plan. By game day, each player knows exactly what his assignment is and how it fits in to the overall team strategy.

Secondly, corporate plans may fail because the key objectives simply do not make sense. They don't make sense because they're often not based on solid evidence. When the evidence is reliable, key decision makers may misinterpret that evidence and formulate

---

[36] Jimmie Butler, "90 Percent of Organizations Fail to Execute Their Strategies Successfully: A White Paper to Help You Avoid Being a Statistic" (IntelliBridge Inc. (Mclean, VA), August 24, 2022.

[37] Rob Sayer, "Strategic Planning and Strategy Execution: Football Does It Better!" Built In Inc. (Chicago, ILL), September 17, 2012.

unwise or unattainable objectives. If your objectives do not make sense, or are unrealistic, you can expect resistance from your employees. Conversely, the regular self-scouts conducted by football coaches ensure a sober assessment of their players' abilities, which lead to attainable objectives that players believe in.

Finally, business plans can fail at the implementation phase because of poor follow-through. It's human nature, to start fast and fizzle faster. Corporate managers often struggle to find ways to keep their employees focused and energized to implement the key objectives of the plan. However, most football coaches instinctively know which buttons to push to get the most out of their players.

I have over thirty years of experience in the business world and coaching football. I am very familiar with quarterly business plans, and football game plans. I assure you; football coaches do a better job of analyzing an opponent and developing a plan. Coaches also are more successful in educating and motivating their players, which increases the odds for successful implementation of the key objectives of the plan.

You may be puzzled why I am stressing the superiority of a football game plan vs. a corporate business plan. I am making these comparisons to not only stress the importance of implementation, but also to explain why I chose to structure our game plan for gaining the assurance of salvation on the football model.

The five obstacles to assurance I have identified are clearly defined, and easy to understand. Your understanding, as well as your assurance, will increase as we discuss each obstacle and how to overcome it. The five obstacles also make sense, as they are based on solid scriptural and scientific research that have been conducted in phases 1–3 of our game plan. Indeed, roughly half of this book is dedicated to laying the necessary groundwork to validate the five key obstacles to the assurance of salvation.

Please understand, I am making these assertions not to be arrogant, but to increase your confidence in the information shared in this book. We are at a very critical stage in our game plan. The methodical and thorough research that was done to distill our game plan down to these five obstacles will be wasted if you don't implement them. Make no mistake, you won't implement them if you don't believe in them. By God's grace, I have successfully navigated through these five obstacles personally, and I want to help you do the same!

Important reminders

As we begin the implementation phase of our game plan, remember that you will be engaging a very powerful spiritual stronghold. You will undoubtedly have to confront the "lion's den," and soldier through the "enchanted ground" at least once as you navigate through each obstacle of assurance. So don't be surprised if you start to get anxious as we discuss certain topics, or mysteriously lose your sense of urgency to gain your assurance. Therefore, it is imperative, as you begin, to put on your spiritual armor by faith. You may even want to read Ephesians 6:10–18 before beginning each new chapter.

Also do not forget to ask the Holy Spirit to guide you into all truth regarding the specific reasons for your struggle with assurance. As I went through this process, the Holy Spirit would first convict me of certain sins of omission or commission that were contributing to my lack of assurance. Only after I confessed and repented of those sins, would the Holy Spirit reveal to me why I committed them in the first place.

The Holy Spirit also revealed deep-seated beliefs that I had about myself and the Word which contributed to seasons of intense doubt concerning my salvation. This divine revelation brought much needed healing to me and was necessary for attaining the assurance of salvation. To that end, the "Mindful Question" at the end of each chapter will help greatly.

Finally, as we walk through each of the obstacles of assurance keep in mind the two key premises of our game-plan.

1. The synergism (negative) of our thoughts, emotions, and actions is a key factor in the formation of spiritual strongholds and increases the difficulty for tearing them down.

2.   The cycle of synergy starts regardless of the initial impetus. Whether our thoughts, emotions, or actions kick start the cycle, the other two will be impacted, and the end result will be the same—the formation of a spiritual stronghold.

For example, in the initial obstacle to be addressed, *uncommitted in walk*, our actions will serve as the initial impetus. Through the synergy discussed, our emotions and thoughts will eventually be impacted. If left to continue unaddressed, this negative cycle of synergy will eventually lead to the spiritual stronghold of assurance-doubt.

In addition to this synergy, the wicked influences of the world, the flesh, and the demonic realm also play key roles in the formation and defense of this stronghold. Below is a TEA graph depicting this process.

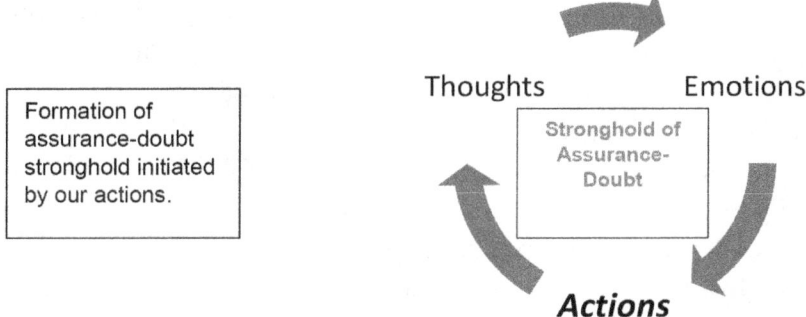

Like a good coach, I will do my level best to keep you motivated until you have understood and overcome each of the five obstacles to the assurance of salvation. Are you ready? Great, then put on your spiritual armor and let's begin then with the first obstacle, *uncommitted in walk*! To introduce the key theme of obedience in our first obstacle, we will look at an account from the life of Alexander the Great.

Importance of obedient actions

Alexander the Great was a daring and brilliant military leader who conquered much of the known world of his day, and he accomplished that remarkable feat while still in his twenties. As legend has it, one day after a particularly fierce battle, a young soldier was brought to Alexander. The boy was handsome and strong and had demonstrated his skill as a fighter in prior combat. However, during an especially brutal campaign, the boy disobeyed the order to advance and was found hiding in a cave. This was a serious offense, and as the officers recounted each of the charges against the young soldier, Alexander became increasingly angry.

However, as Alexander looked on this young boy his visage changed from anger to compassion. He calmly said to him, "Soldier, what is your name?" With his head down, the boy whispered, "Alexander." In an instant Alexander's anger returned, "What did you say?" The lad snapped to attention. "Alexander, sir." The great general was now furious, and shouted, "What is your name?" Stammering and stuttering the boy said, "Al, Al, Alexander, sir." The king then seized the young man, looked him dead in the eye, and said to him, "Soldier, change your conduct or change your name!"

It is unknown if this story from the life of Alexander the Great is true or legend. However, what is certain, is the supreme importance of its underlying principles: duty, honor, and obedience. As Christians, we bear an infinitely more noble name than Alexander. Christ is the omnipotent Son of God, and Captain of Host. It is our duty and honor to obey Him.

You may be wondering why I chose to begin discussion with the obstacle I placed fourth in my list, "*uncommitted in walk.*" The short answer is that it's the easiest to comprehend. Actions are more tangible than thoughts or emotions. They produce consequences that are obvious to self-diagnose or with the help of others. Actions are also easier to address and correct. One can normally stop a behavior faster than the thoughts, and feelings, associated with it.

However, the main reason for starting with this obstacle is the supreme importance of obedience. As Bonhoeffer said, one act of obedience is better than one hundred sermons. Jesus said if you love Me, you will keep My commandments (John 14:15). Paul and Samuel link obedience directly with worship, while John affirms that obedience demonstrates the genuineness of our faith.

> I appeal to you therefore, brothers, by the mercies of God, to present your bodies as a living sacrifice, holy and acceptable to God, which is your spiritual worship. (Romans 12:1)

> And Samuel said, "Has the LORD as great delight in burnt offerings and sacrifices, as in obeying the voice of the LORD? Behold, to obey is better than sacrifice, and to listen than the fat of rams" (1 Samuel 15:22)

> Whoever says "I know him" but does not keep his commandments is a liar, and the truth is not in him. (1 John 2:4)

2 Peter 1:5–10
Actions and assurance

In addition to linking obedience with worship and faith, there are also many passages in Scripture that demonstrate the relationship between our obedient actions with the attaining and maintaining of assurance. Second Peter 1:5–10, listed in its entirety below, is one such passage that shows the linkage between our Christian walk and the assurance of salvation.

> [5] For this very reason, make every effort to supplement your faith with virtue, and virtue with knowledge, [6] and knowledge with self-control, and self-control with steadfastness, and steadfastness with godliness, [7] and godliness with brotherly affection, and brotherly affection

with love. [8] For if these qualities are yours and are increasing, they keep you from being ineffective or unfruitful in the knowledge of our Lord Jesus Christ. [9] For whoever lacks these qualities is so nearsighted that he is blind, having forgotten that he was cleansed from his former sins. [10] Therefore, brothers, be all the more diligent to confirm your calling and election, for if you practice these qualities you will never fall. (2 Peter 1:5–10)

In verses 5–8, Peter lays out a series of directives expected of all believers. In fact, Peter says, "make every effort" to add these things to our faith. Peter identifies seven separate tasks believers must do, and it should not be surprising by now, that they all have to do with our thoughts, emotions, and actions!

Regarding our thoughts, Peter says to increase your knowledge. Of course, we do that by studying the Word of God. As for our emotions, brotherly affection and love is the goal to achieve. However, clueing us in to the main thrust of his argument in this passage, Peter not only leads his list of seven directives with an example of action, but also more than half of his commands are directly linked to expected Christian behavior.

As for our actions, virtue, or moral excellence is first on Peter's list, followed by self-control, steadfastness, and godliness. In addition, it's important to note Peter's emphasis on the urgency to act in his opening and closing of this passage. He begins in verse 5 with, *"Make every effort to supplement your faith,"* and closes in verse 10 with, *"Be all the more diligent to confirm your calling and election."*

Peter is writing the very words of God, and thus God affirms that only fervent action on our part will strengthen and solidify our faith and assurance. Regarding this fervency, the great Scottish preacher, Alexander MacLaren, offers his own insights.

Hence we gather that no Christian growth is possible unless a man gives his mind to it.

> Dawdlers will do nothing. There must be fervour
> if there is to be growth. The heated bar of iron
> will go through the obstacle which the cold one
> will never penetrate.[38]

Even the allusions to our thoughts (knowledge) and emotions (brotherly affection and love) are swept up in this same call to action. Yet Peter's view in this regard is not unique in Scripture. Regarding our knowledge of the Word, Paul commanded Timothy to, "Study to shew thyself approved unto God, a workman that needeth not to be ashamed, rightly dividing the word of truth" (2 Tim. 2:15 KJV). Diligent, responsible Bible study can be hard work. However, without such effort, error and even heresy is possible. Regarding brotherly affection and love, both James and John understood that such emotions must also be validated by action.

> If a brother or sister is poorly clothed and
> lacking in daily food, and one of you says to
> them, "Go in peace, be warmed and filled," with-
> out giving them the things needed for the body,
> what good is that? (James 2:15–16)

> Little children, let us not love in word or
> talk but in deed and in truth. (1 John 3:18)

Peter couldn't be more emphatic to move us to action because he knew what was at stake. In verses 9–10, Peter gives the sobering consequences if we fail to heed his commands; we will become ineffective and unfruitful. Peter also says that those who lack these qualities are so nearsighted that they are, for all intents and purposes,

---

[38] Alexander MacLaren, "The Power of Diligence (2 Peter 1:5)." Blue Letter Bible; February 17, 2022; Web. March 11, 2023; https://www.blueletterbible.org/comm/maclaren_alexander/expositions-of-holy-scripture/2-peter/the-power-of-diligence.cfm.

blind. MacArthur discusses the spiritual significance of the term nearsightedness that Peter uses.

> The blind believer is nearsighted. He has spiritual myopia. The Greek modifying participle here gives us the word myopia. Myopia is a condition of the eye in which parallel rays are focused in front of the retina. Nearsighted people focus right in front of them, but the farther out they look, the worse their vision becomes. Distant things are out of focus. Believers who are not fruitful go spiritually blind because their perspective is limited. They focus on the earth and the things of the earth—the passing fads and fashions of the day. By the time they try to look to eternity, it is so out of focus for them that they can't perceive it. They are victims of spiritual myopia.[39]

I said way back in chapter 1 that personal growth in the faith is stunted, and sustained diligence in Christian service is impossible, for believers who lack assurance. I made that statement based on this very passage of Scripture. Peter concludes that spiritual blindness, characterized by an ineffective and fruitless life, will eventually lead to spiritual amnesia. If believers do not take their faith seriously, they will eventually doubt their own conversion; "*having forgotten that he was cleansed from his former sins,*" (2 Peter 1:9b).

In other words, disobedience regarding the directives of verses 5–8 will rob a believer of the assurance of salvation. Again, it is important to stress that Peter is writing to Christians, and that dereliction in their obedience will have consequences. Namely an ineffective and unfruitful walk culminating in the spiritual stronghold of assurance-doubt. As opposed to Alexander's; "Change your conduct, or change your name!" Peter commands, "Change your conduct, or you'll forget your name!"

---

[39] Ibid.

Given the great relevance that applying these seven items to our faith has on our assurance, it behooves us to understand what Peter means by each. Also, to fully grasp Peter's teaching, we need to consider why he chose to list these graces in the order he did. What follows then, is a brief explanation of each of the items we are to add to our faith and how they are related by their arrangement. I will also add comments on practical ways I was able to apply these principles in my own struggle with assurance.

There is a clear pattern for the way Peter arranges his list. Each item serves as a steppingstone for the next item on his list. However, the list is not rigidly sequential. For example, Peter is not suggesting that you shouldn't start focusing on knowledge until virtuous behavior is checked off the list. Rather, each successive grace completes and clarifies the one that came before. Thus, the preceding graces find their fruition and purpose within the successive ones.

Peter was using a common literary device, called a sorites. Paul used this long-chain argument in Romans 8:28–30 (the golden chain of redemption) as well. In the case of 2 Peter 1:5–9, it may be helpful to visualize the sorites with successive circles beginning with virtue and culminating with love that fulfills and encloses everything. Thus, each of the first six graces find their complete actualization in the grace of love. Below is the illustration of the sorites for 2 Peter 1:5–9.

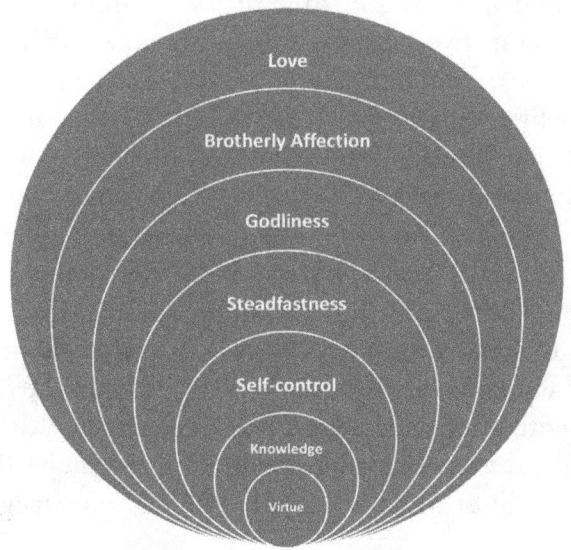

Graces 1–2: Virtue and Knowledge

Peter begins the list with virtue, or ethical behavior that is above reproach. One might have predicted that a passage on growing in faith and assurance would have begun with the knowledge of the Scriptures. However, Peter chose instead to focus first on the importance of Christian behavior. We have already hinted at three reasons he may have made this choice. First; is the premium the Bible places on obedience. Second, he may have led with virtue to foreshadow the dominant theme of action in the passage. The third reason could be the same rationale that I had for beginning with the obstacle; *uncommitted in walk*. Namely, that actions are often easier to address than thoughts and emotions.

However, a fourth reason for leading with virtue as opposed to knowledge becomes apparent when one considers that roughly two-thirds of the New Testament was already completed and in circulation by the time Peter wrote his epistles, not to mention the entire Old Testament. One could surmise, then, that according to Peter, the first order of business for a Christian is to put into practice the things you already know to be true. All these reasons may have played a role, but the full meaning for starting with virtue becomes clear when one understands who Peter is writing to and their unique circumstances.

Peter's audience was a mixture of Jewish and Gentile believers who were living in five separate Roman provinces; Pontus, Galatia, Cappadocia, Asia, and Bithynia (1 Peter 1:1). The Greco-Roman culture of the first century was characterized by rampant idolatry and gross immorality (Romans 1:16–28; 1 Corinthians 5:1–11; Galatians 4:8–10; 1 Thessalonians 4:3–7) which had a profound impact on the early church. Perhaps Peter begins with virtue, because of the decadent society in which these believers lived. Remember, virtue does not just mean moral behavior; the word also conveys the courage that it takes to stand strong in your convictions in the face of great pressure and temptation. To live a virtuous life amid the temptations of the first century required a great deal of courage.

I have listed several possible reasons Peter began his list with the grace of virtue, all of which still apply today in our struggle to gain assurance. However, central to each of those reasons is the primacy of obedience, the importance of which has been sadly dismissed in recent years.

There has been an unfortunate movement in the past few decades that asserts that a person can accept Christ as Savior but not as Lord. That notion is foreign to the Bible. Christ is both, and our obedience to Him as our Lord and Master is essential to the faith and directly impacts our assurance. MacArthur picks up on the centrality of obedience for the Christian.

> When a person comes to Christ to receive salvation, it is a call to obedience. In fact, the apostle Paul even called salvation the obedience of faith, a faith that obeys, a faith that submits, a faith that follows, a faith that subscribes itself to all the commands that God has given.
>
> Such obedience is an essential component in our Christian living. It is foundational to our power, our joy, our usefulness and our blessing. And we would all acknowledge that, that coming to Jesus Christ for salvation was an affirmation that I will obey Him.[40]

Despite what liberal theologians and pastors may say, the consequences of living your life as if Christ was not Lord will be just as Peter says—an ineffective unfruitful life with no assurance. Moreover, the world we live in rivals or surpasses the decadence of Greco-Roman society and requires courage on our part to live virtuously. We too, must have the same sense of urgency to add virtue to our faith. Without virtue assurance is impossible.

However, there were two other influences, more dangerous than that posed by the Greco-Roman culture. Sadly, those influences came from inside the church itself; the heretical teachings of the Judaizers

---

[40] John MacArthur, "Love: The Key to Obedience," Grace to You (gty.org) (All rights reserved. Used by permission"). October 10, 1991, 80–92.

and the Gnostics. So Peter moves on from the grace of virtue to knowledge, and for good reason!

The Judaizers were ostensibly Jewish Christians who asserted that Gentile believers had to conform to the Mosaic law. Thus, they demanded new Gentile converts be circumcised, observe Jewish Sabbath and dietary laws, as well as celebrate Jewish feast days.

The Judaizers were a formidable group, that despite being denounced at a special council held in Jerusalem (Acts 15), still brazenly sought to spread their heresy. They were so forceful, that even Peter was intimidated by their presence, for which he was corrected publicly by Paul (Galatians 2:11–14).

Conversely, Gnostic heresies of the first century and beyond were much harder to define than the teachings of the Judaizers, primarily because there were so many different forms of Gnosticism. However, at their core, these false teachers taught the same heresy; faith in Christ was not enough for salvation.

The Gnostics believed that there was secret knowledge necessary for salvation that only angels or enlightened Gnostic teachers could impart. They also believed that the material universe was evil, and so they practiced extreme forms of asceticism, forbidding certain behaviors, foods, etc. Other Gnostic heretics taught the exact opposite, and espoused licentious practices under the guise of Christian liberty.

The teachings of the Judaizers and the Gnostics was a great danger to the early church. Entire epistles of the New Testament were written primarily to refute these heresies, and many other New Testament books included warnings against the ever-present threat posed by these false teachers. In light of this doctrinal threat, Peter says to add to their virtue the grace of knowledge.

Just as federal agents are trained to spot counterfeit bills by studying the look and feel of authentic currency, we need to study the Bible to spot false teaching. King Solomon said there is nothing new under the sun, and repackaged forms of Gnosticism and Judaizing exist to this day.

Contemporary churches infiltrated by such false teachings always seek to add their own set of rules to the Gospel. In such congregations these man-made rules can become the litmus test for genuine salvation, or at the very least, a barometer for "maturity and obedience" in the faith.

Like the Judaizers and Gnostics, leaders of such churches seek power, prestige, and control, which they secure by their "rules." The rules vary depending upon the church, and unfortunately it is impossible to list all of them. However, they always include things we can eat or drink, the clothes we can wear, what we can read or listen to, and even how or when we may worship. Below are my top ten rules to be aware of:

1. Women must wear dresses and men must have their hair cut short.
2. Doctrine divides—only the heart matters, so no teaching on truth or sin is welcome.
3. Theaters are off-limits as is all contemporary music.
4. Total abstinence regarding alcohol and tobacco is required.
5. If you don't speak in tongues, you are either unsaved, deceived, or not "Spirit filled."
6. Biblical truth cannot be understood by reason but only through special mystical intuition.
7. The Bible "we" use is the true Word of God. Reading any other translation is sinful.
8. If you are not, "healthy and wealthy," then you don't have enough faith.
9. You can't do any recreational activity on Sunday.
10. You must not be educated in a public school or secular university.

Churches adopting such rules often seek to govern virtually every aspect of one's life, and their leaders and laity intimidate and slander any who dare to question them. However, Paul says it is our duty to guard the faith and our assurance by resisting those who would seek to disqualify us based upon extrabiblical rules that elevate men rather than Christ.

> Therefore let no one pass judgment on you in questions of food and drink, or with regard to a festival or a new moon or a Sabbath.
>
> These are a shadow of the things to come, but the substance belongs to Christ.
>
> Let no one disqualify you, insisting on asceticism and worship of angels, going on in detail about visions, puffed up without reason by his sensuous mind,
>
> and not holding fast to the Head, from whom the whole body, nourished and knit together through its joints and ligaments, grows with a growth that is from God.
>
> If with Christ you died to the elemental spirits of the world, why, as if you were still alive in the world, do you submit to regulations—
>
> "Do not handle, Do not taste, Do not touch" (referring to things that all perish as they are used)—according to human precepts and teachings?
>
> These have indeed an appearance of wisdom in promoting self-made religion and asceticism and severity to the body, but they are of no value in stopping the indulgence of the flesh. (Colossians 2:16–23)

Every church has the right to unify around a certain set of convictions and practices, and all believers should vigorously defend their right to do so. However, no church has the right to elevate their "rules" to the authority of the Word of God. Remember Jesus said, "if you love Me obey My commandments"—not somebody else's!

Such false teachings invariably lead to the extremes of legalism on the one hand and license on the other. Both extremes will never produce lasting assurance. However, false teaching can also lead to lethargy. Christians can be become discouraged and disillusioned by the proliferation of legalistic or licentious teaching and practices within the Church. As a result, genuine believers may gradually disconnect from the process of spiritual growth and eventually lose their assurance as well.

Legalism, license, and lethargy are inevitable when man-made rules are substituted for biblical virtue and knowledge. This substitution of God's truth for the errors of men always results in a weakened and distorted walk with Christ, and churches characterized by such practices will have a very short life span. This is why Peter is so insistent that all effort be given to add knowledge to virtue. In light of that importance, I will close our discussion of virtue and knowledge with a few roadblocks to be aware of and some practical ways in which they can be avoided.

First, I will warn of the strong temptation for those struggling with assurance to first fall into legalistic behaviors. This makes sense considering the synergy that exists within our thoughts, emotions, and behaviors. Living an overly ascetic lifestyle may produce emotions that counter the fear associated with assurance-doubt. However, that peace will be short-lived, because the behaviors are not based on the truth of Scripture. The fear and doubt will return. I went down that road, and I have witnessed other Christians do the same. It is a frustrating dead-end that eventually leads to lethargy and perhaps even license. It is only when you totally grasp the promises of God concerning salvation, and understand what behaviors God does require, will a lasting peace regarding your salvation be achieved.

So what then did Peter mean by virtue? Is it, as the old saying goes, "Don't drink, smoke, and chew, or go out with girls who do"? For many believers, that tongue-in-cheek phrase is not far off the mark in defining their Christian ethic.

I mentioned that football coaches are very adept at distilling mountains of data down to a few key objectives. Focusing on what really matters, is what allows a coach to make sound offensive or defensive calls in the thirty seconds or less that he has between plays.

Similarly, theologians tell us that there are over six hundred specific commands in the Bible. That is a lot of data to analyze! It turns out that several authors of Scripture would make very good football coaches as they also had a way of getting to the heart of the matter with regards to our behaviors.

Though all Scripture is important (2 Timothy 3:16), in my struggle with assurance I guided my actions primarily on a few passages of Scripture that capture the essence of the Christian ethic. They remain my "North Star" verses to keep my actions grounded in what really matters. I believe you will find these commands much more difficult to obey than refraining from going to the theater, enjoying a cigar with a friend, or having a glass of wine with your spouse!

"North Star" verses

1. Did not your father eat and drink and do justice and righteousness? Then it was well with him. He judged the cause of the poor and needy; then it was well. Is not this to know me? declares the LORD. (Jeremiah 22:15b-16)

2. He has told you, O man, what is good; and what does the LORD require of you but to do justice, and to love kindness, and to walk humbly with your God? (Micah 6:8)

3. And he said to him, "You shall love the Lord your God with all your heart and with all your soul and with all your mind. This is the great and first commandment. And a second is like it: You shall love your neighbor as yourself. On these two commandments depend all the Law and the Prophets." (Matthew 22:37–40)

4. "So whatever you wish that others would do to you, do also to them, for this is the Law and the Prophets. (Matthew 7:12)

5. And he said to all, "If anyone would come after me, let him deny himself and take up his cross daily and follow me. For whoever would save his life will lose it, but whoever loses his life for my sake will save it. (Luke 9:23–24)

Finally, it is very important for my fellow believers who deal with OCD, to recognize that the compulsions you have developed to ease the emotional and mental distress associated with assurance-doubt are counterproductive. Though your motives and efforts are no doubt genuine, the stronghold of assurance-doubt will only be made stronger the longer you engage in such compulsions.

There is a saying that those in the OCD community live by, and it is, "Don't feed the monster"! By performing whatever rituals, you have developed to ease your fears and worries, you are only feeding the monster and making your condition worse. Moreover, these compulsions are not examples of biblical virtue or obedience. Focus your attention instead on the behaviors God deems important through His Word and put those into practice.

Graces 3–5: Self-control, steadfastness, and godliness

As noted, Peter's audience knew right from wrong with regards to virtuous behavior but needed to add knowledge to discern that the behaviors being condemned by the heretics were unfounded in Scripture. However, once this knowledge of adiaphorous or allowable behavior was obtained, Peter states that it must be tempered by self-control.

Peter references the writings of Paul in his second epistle (2 Peter 3:15–16), and I can't help but wonder if Paul's theology did not influence Peter to position the grace of self-control immediately following virtue and knowledge.

Paul dealt with a wide range of behaviors that were causing confusion, strife, and division within the church. These were complicated questions concerning marriage practices, foods, worship and various other issues that required divine wisdom to discern.

In Romans, 1 Corinthians, and elsewhere, Paul explains the relationship of self-control to our knowledge of Scripture, especially in areas that are often mistakenly regarded as sinful practices. According to Paul, there are three main considerations that should govern our self-control in such contested areas.

1. *Everything by faith:* Faith, used in this context by Paul is a conviction of judgment, a certainty that a particular behavior does not violate the Scriptures or Christ's will for your life. Therefore, if you personally believe something is sinful (though in reality it is not), Paul says not to do it. For all intents and purposes, your engagement in such a practice would be a sin for you and wound your weak conscience (Romans 14:23).

2. *Everything with fealty:* Fealty refers to loyalty and allegiance to which one is bound by duty. We have one Master and Lord, Jesus Christ (Matthew 23:8–10; John 13:13; 1 Corinthians 8:6). Thus, if you become mastered by any practice, even one that in and of itself is not sinful, it becomes sinful to you (Romans 14:22–23; 1 Cor. 6:12).

3. *Everything in filialness:* Filialness refers to the love and respect a son or daughter is to show to their parents. With regards to our liberty, we are to show our brothers and sisters in Christ the same deference a child would for the wishes of his parent. Thus, Paul says that if your engagement in a non-sinful practice will destroy the faith of a weaker brother, refrain from doing it in their presence (Romans 14:20–21; 1 Corinthians 8:11–13).

Paul is clear—in relation to ourselves, the Lord, and our brothers and sisters—we are to exercise self-control with regards to our Christian liberty. However, to those who would seek to enslave us with their un-biblical rules we are not to give in an inch!

> Stand fast therefore in the liberty wherewith
> Christ hath made us free and be not entangled
> again with the yoke of bondage. (Galatians 5:1)

In our game plan for assurance, consider Paul's three guiding principles for self-control. Is your conscience bothered by any behaviors? Has anything mastered you? Are you protective of the faith of your fellow Christians? Refusal to exercise Paul's three principles of self-control in areas where the Bible allows for liberty may eventually manifest in unambiguous sin which will adversely affect our assurance. Self-control must be taken seriously and consistently applied to our faith. Therefore, Peter says to add to our self-control, the grace of steadfastness.

Warren Buffet, the billionaire investor wisely said, "It takes twenty years to build a reputation, and five minutes to ruin it." Sadly, many believers have shipwrecked their faith and testimony because of a lack of steadfastness in the practice of self-control.

The Greek word for *steadfastness* used in this passage is; ὑπομονή (hoop-om-on-ay). Some Bibles translate the word as "patience" or "perseverance." Whether the word is translated as *steadfastness*, *patience*, or *perseverance*, the underlying prerequisite of consistency remains.

It's important to remember how Peter is constructing this list. Each successive grace we are to add to our faith not only has its own inherent importance, but also completes the full meaning of the grace that preceded it. Thus, Peter affirms it is not enough to exhibit biblical self-control, to study the Scriptures, and to live virtuously, every now and then. We must be consistent. Paul told Timothy to be ready in season and out of season (2 Timothy 4:2). In other words, we need to be consistently steadfast whether the task at hand is easy or hard, or whether we feel like it or not.

Let's be honest, being consistent is hard work. Consistency requires discipline and commitment. However, consistent effort is made easier when a clear goal is set before us. The goal for Peter's entire list—virtue, knowledge, self-control, etc.—is a fruitful and effective life with the full assurance of salvation. Being steadfast in adding these items to our faith is necessary to achieve that goal. Yet even our steadfastness needs to be completed by another grace, godliness.

Vince Lombardi, the legendary football coach of the Green Bay Packers once said, "Practice does not make perfect, only perfect practice makes perfect." He made that statement to guard his players from just going through the motions. Perhaps this is what Peter has in mind here when he says to add to our steadfastness, the grace of godliness.

Godliness is a term that is not used much in our day. It refers to a devotion to God born out of a reverent fear and love for God. Godliness is characterized by a desire to please God in every aspect of our lives. This is the driving factor and purpose for our steadfastness in the faith.

The grace of godliness completes and perfects our steadfastness, it is "perfect practice" as Coach Lombardi would say. Without godliness, our walk with the Lord can easily fall into a series of passionless rote exercises, that will not spur us on to the two final graces we are to add to our faith: The capstones of brotherly affection and love.

Graces 6–7: Brotherly affection and love

All the items that Peter has mentioned thus far are gathering momentum like a tsunami ready to make landfall in the final two graces of brotherly affection and love. The five preceding graces are needed to equip us as individuals to pour out brotherly affection and love to others. Thus, with these last two additions to our faith, Peter is shifting the primary focus from an internal one to an external.

At first glance it may appear that these final two graces mean the same thing. However, the distinction is found in the recipients to whom they are applied. The Greek word for *brotherly affection* is φιλαδελφία (philadelphia). It is used six times in the New Testament and always refers to the love that Christians are to have for their brothers and sisters in the faith.

As believers we are each born of God (John 1:12–13) and are brothers and sisters in the Lord. Therefore, I do not believe it is a stretch to apply Paul's charge to take care of our earthly relatives (1 Timothy 5:8) to our spiritual family as well. Indeed, Paul said that though we are to do good to all men, we are to prioritize the church.

> As we have therefore opportunity, let us do
> good unto all men, especially unto them who are
> of the household of faith. (Galatians 6:10)

Though we prioritize our earthly and spiritual families, we do not stop there. So Peter concludes his list with love. The word used here is, ἀγάπη (ag-ah'-pay). It refers to God's love for all of humanity as well as our love for God. It is the highest form of love. Every grace previously mentioned prepares us to display this kind of love. Jesus said, loving God and our fellow man are the two great commandments (Matthew 22:36–40) and the distinguishing characteristic of His disciples.

> By this shall all men know that ye are my
> disciples, if ye have love one to another. (John
> 13:35 KJV)

The love of others, even those we deem enemies, is our duty as Christians. Jesus confirmed that in the Sermon on the Mount, and powerfully illustrated it in the parable of the Good Samaritan. Only this type of self-sacrificing love mimics the love of God and demonstrates our maturity and completeness in the faith (Matthew 5:43–48).

We resist obeying the command to love in this way because it goes against our fallen nature. To be truthful, many aspects of our calling as believers are difficult and unpalatable, but it is the cross we must take up. Accepting this reality requires a determined mindset to put off the "old man" and live in the power of the Spirit. However, we often govern our obedience to Christ according to our feelings. The old mantra of the 1970s, "If it feels good, do it," has been replaced in this generation with, "If it doesn't feel good, don't do it"!

That said, the love Peter references must be understood in its verb form—tangible demonstrations of good deeds done for our fellow man despite the feelings we have for them. Yet the concept of synergy tells us that our actions will produce emotions. It's true we may never feel fondness for certain people, but when we demonstrate the love of God to them, we will feel compassion for them, and experience the peaceable fruit of righteousness ourselves.

It is remarkable that when we are obedient to love in this regard, the resulting compassion and peace we feel has a profound impact on the felt weight of our cross. Perhaps this is part of what Jesus meant when He said, "My yoke is easy and My burden is light" (Matthew 11:28–30).

Remember, the graces of brotherly affection and love are to be present in all of our relationship, beginning with our earthly and spiritual family and extending to each person God puts in our lives. According to Peter, our treatment of others is the true barometer of our faith and will have a profound impact on our assurance. Therefore, in our game plan for gaining the assurance of salvation we need to soberly consider all of our interpersonal relationships.

To begin, assess your relationship with your parents. Do you honor them (Exodus 20:12), by spending time with them, helping them, speaking well of them, etc.? How about your brothers, sisters, and children? Are there any unresolved issues with your siblings that you have not done your due diligence to rectify (Matthew 5:23–24)? For fathers and husbands, do you exasperate your children (Ephesians 6:4) or fail to love and cherish your wives (Ephesians 5:25). For wives, do you love and respect your husbands (Eph. 5:33)? Remember our familial relationships and responsibilities are critically important aspects of our faith.

But if any provide not for his own, and specially for those of his own house, he hath denied

the faith, and is worse than an infidel. (1 Timothy
5:8 KJV)

Moving on to our spiritual family, how is your relationship with
fellow Christians? Do you belong to a church, regularly attend its
services (Hebrews 10:25) and financially support it (Matthew 23:23;
Mark 12:17; 1 Corinthians 16:2)? Is there any brother or sister in the
faith whom you have not forgiven from your heart (Ephesians 4:32;
Colossians 3:13)?

Finally, consider your relationships with your friends, neigh-
bors, coworkers, etc. Do you treat them as you would like to be
treated (Matthew 7:12)? Do you act justly and mercifully towards
them (Jeremiah 22:15b-16; Micah 6:8). Remember, this is not about
feelings, we are not commanded to like everyone, but we are commanded to pray for them and to do good to them (1 Timothy 2:1–2;
Galatians 6:10). Showing the agape love of God to our fellow man,
is the mark that we are truly adding all the graces to our faith that
Peter commands.

Final thoughts

All seven graces we are to add to our faith concern our thoughts,
emotions, and actions and therefore work synergistically together to
make us effective and fruitful in our walk as Christians and produces
the full assurance of salvation. However, Peter tells us the addition
of these graces requires fervent action on our part. God will certainly
help us, but we must play our part. Paul told the Philippians the
same thing.

> Wherefore, my beloved, as ye have always
> obeyed, not as in my presence only, but now
> much more in my absence, work out your own
> salvation with fear and trembling. For it is God
> which worketh in you both to will and to do of
> his good pleasure. (Philippians 2:12–13 KJV)

Peter and Paul are not the only New Testament writers that makes this connection. James and John arrive at the same conclusion. All four men link our actions as believers with our conscious experience of assurance.

> [22] But be doers of the word, and not hearers only, deceiving yourselves. [23] For if anyone is a hearer of the word and not a doer, he is like a man who looks intently at his natural face in a mirror. [24] For he looks at himself and goes away and at once forgets what he was like. [25] But the one who looks into the perfect law, the law of liberty, and perseveres, being no hearer who forgets but a doer who acts, he will be blessed in his doing. (James 1:22–25)

> Little children, let us not love in word or talk but in deed and in truth. By this we shall know that we are of the truth and reassure our heart before him. (1 John 3:18–19)

The Bible is very clear that our actions must be congruent with our faith. When they are not, the consequences are an ineffectual life characterized by self-doubt. Sam Goldwyn, the famous Hollywood mogul, once said, "The greatest gap that exists in life is between knowing and doing." If the gap between our knowledge of Scripture and our obedience in applying that knowledge is cavernous, we can expect little to no assurance. According to the Bible then, "Goldwyn's gap," is directly proportional to the assurance we experience!

When we neglect to add the seven graces to our faith that Peter identifies, our actions to one degree or another will devolve into legalism, license or lethargy. If not addressed, such disobedience will eventually have a negative impact on our thoughts and emotions, leading to the spiritual stronghold of assurance-doubt. In such cases, a return to a committed life is the remedy. However, as we return to a committed life of obedience there are some very important caveats to consider.

To begin, one must be aware that the driving purpose of our good works is not for our benefit. We don't live obediently solely to get the assurance we crave. That said, remember from our discussion of David's interest for Saul's reward, that it is impossible not to have multiple desires at the same time. Therefore, be obedient because it's your duty (Luke 17:10), but also enjoy the assurance that you will receive as a reward.

Secondly, Jesus also made it emphatically clear that our good works are never to be done for personal glory (Matthew 6:1). Our good works are for others to see, so they can glorify God, "In the same way, let your light shine before others, so that they may see your good works and give glory to your Father who is in heaven (Matthew 5:16). Paul tells the Corinthians the same.

> So whether you eat or drink, or whatever you do, do all to the glory of God. Give no offense to Jews or to Greeks or to the church of God, just as I try to please everyone in everything I do, not seeking my own advantage, but that of many, that they may be saved. (1 Corinthians 10:31)

Finally, one must be aware of the driving force behind a return to obedience. Is it simply to appease a perceived angry God? If so, James says that is not, "looking into the perfect law of liberty" (James 1:25). In fact, it smacks of paganism, or an attempt at works-righteousness. Such errant thinking and motivation will invariably cause one to misinterpret clear themes and passages in the Bible. For example, an often misunderstood passage is Philippians 2:12–13. When Paul told the Philippians to work out their own salvation with fear and trembling, he was using a common Jewish idiom that meant with reverence, diligence, gratefulness, and awe (Psalms 2:11; 2 Corinthians 7:15; Ephesians 2:5). He was not charging believers to live in a constant state of anxiety and nervousness.

Acts of obedience done in a spirit of fearful appeasement, no matter how pious, will not produce true lasting assurance. Instead of dismantling the spiritual stronghold of assurance-doubt, such obedience will only make it stronger. Obedience spawned from fear and error as opposed to love and truth will never produce genuine assurance. It is this impossibility that will serve as the segue to the next obstacle, *unrestored in emotions*.

However, before moving on to the next chapter, prayerfully consider what role if any, the destructive dangers of legalism, license, and lethargy that comprise the obstacle of *uncommitted in walk*, contributes to your lack of assurance. In that regard, completing the "Mindful Question" will help you to make an accurate assessment.

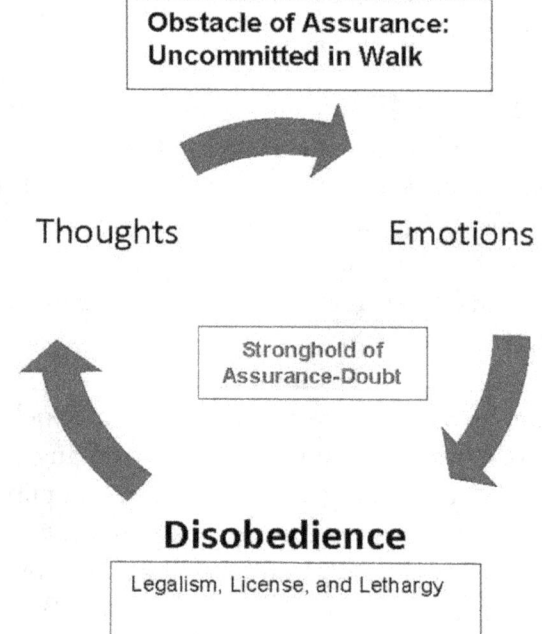

Mindful question

Prayerfully assess your own fervency to mature in the Faith by completing the Self-scout below.

Graces to add to your faith	Self-Scout: Soberly assess your progress in each grace. Ask the Holy Spirit to reveal if your negligence in adding any of these items to your faith is contributing to your lack of assurance.
Virtue	
Knowledge	
Self-control	
Steadfastness	
Godliness	
Brotherly affection	
Love	

8

GAME PLAN—PHASE 4: IMPLEMENTATION

UNRESTORED IN EMOTIONS

There are only two emotions: love and fear.
—Elisabeth Kubler-Ross

The power of fear

In the previous chapter we saw how our actions can serve as the impetus to start the cycle of synergy leading to the spiritual stronghold of assurance-doubt. In this chapter, we will examine how our emotions can initiate this process (see TEA graph below).

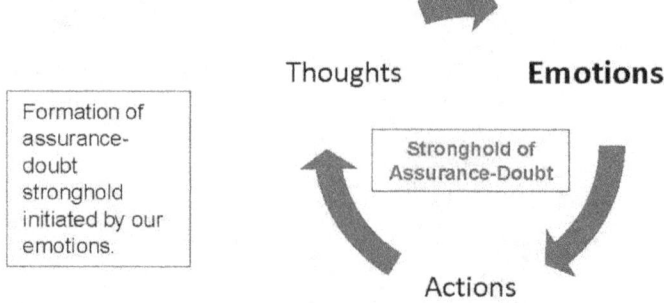

The opening chapter quote was made by the late Dr. Elisabeth Kubler-Ross, a brilliant psychiatrist; whom *Time* magazine named one of the "100 Most Important Thinkers" of the twentieth century. Of course, the point Kubler-Ross was making is that all positive emotions are born from love, while all negative emotions originate from fear. From love, springs peace, joy, happiness, etc., whereas fear spawns guilt, shame, hate, and all other destructive emotions. We saw in the previous chapter that for assurance to be achieved we must be controlled by the final grace of love. Thus, when assurance is absent, love is absent, and fear is the dominant emotion. Therefore, fear must be thoroughly understood and managed for assurance to be achieved.

It's important to note as we begin our discussion of fear, that in and of itself the emotion of fear is not sinful. In fact, fear in its proper place is extremely beneficial as a deterrent to engaging in all manner of impulsive and foolish behaviors (Prov. 22:3; 27:12). However, fear can become sinful when it prevents us from doing what is right or what we are commanded to do (Revelation 21:8), or if we fear something or someone more than we fear God (Isaiah 8:13; Luke 12:4–5). Both sinful reactions to fear will be a temptation for you as you progress through your game plan for assurance.

I mentioned earlier that you will have to face the "lion's den" and journey through the "enchanted ground" as you engage in the process of tearing down the spiritual stronghold of assurance-doubt. From my experience, the bewitchment of the "enchanted ground" was the tactic Satan used most to prevent me from overcoming the obstacle of *uncommitted in walk*.

However, overcoming the obstacle of *unrestored in emotions* required me to enter the "lion's den" and honestly deal with the memories, emotions, and consequences of regrettable sins I committed, as well as the hurtful actions of others toward me. Therefore, as you face the "lion's den" expect to encounter some fear and anxiety. More importantly, be aware of the following three ways fear can lead you into sin and undermine your efforts to gain assurance. These are the three dangers of fear:

1. Fear can be a source of doubt that leads us into sin.

2. Fear can be a source of distraction that leads us into sin.
3. Fear can devolve into destructive emotions that can lead us into sin.

The remainder of this chapter will discuss these three detrimental effects of fear from a biblical and psychological perspective. I will give examples from Scripture where these effects of fear overcame some and were overcome by others. Let the former serve as a caution for us, and the latter as an encouragement. I will begin with a successful navigation of fear's ability to cause doubt by a great hero of the faith.

Fear causes doubt: John the Baptist

Fear is a powerful emotion. It not only serves as the fountainhead for all negative emotions, but it also has the ability to seize control of our mind and lead us into the two aforementioned areas of sin. One way fear can accomplish this is by causing paralyzing doubts of the things we know to be true. Examples of fear causing such doubts are replete in Scriptures. David saying in his heart, "I shall perish one day by the hand of Saul" (1 Samuel 27:1), Elijah fleeing from Jezebel (1 Kings 19:3), and Peter sinking under the waves (Matthew 14:30) are just three examples from the lives of great men of faith.

To add more credence to fear's power in this regard, the three events just mentioned, occurred immediately after God showed His unmistakable power and presence in the lives of these three men. Time does not permit a full development of each of these accounts. However, an example of this phenomenon, that is, the emotion of fear leading to doubt and a lack of assurance, will be developed fully from the life of John the Baptist.

According to Jesus, John was the greatest man to ever live. When Jesus offers His estimation of a man, it is not just another man's opinion. It is a fact. No man was greater than John the Baptist, not Alexander the Great, Nebuchadnezzar, Julius Caesar, or any renowned man of secular history. Even the patriarchs and heroes of the Old Testament did not rise to John's level. Certainly, John's greatness was linked to his monumental mission of preparing the way of the Lord (Mark 1:3). Nonetheless, in his personal character John was in a class by himself. Yet we will see that the power of fear can impact even the best of men.

At the height of John's ministry, he had no doubts regarding Christ, boldly proclaiming, *"Behold the lamb of God who takes away the sins of the world"* (John 1:29). God Himself bore witness to John personally regarding Jesus. This remarkable experience convinced John of Christ's true identity. Listen to John's own testimony regarding Jesus.

> I myself did not know him, but He who sent me to baptize with water said to me, "He on whom you see the Spirit descend and remain, this is He who baptizes with the Holy Spirit." And I have seen and have borne witness that this is the Son of God. (John 1:33–34)

However, not long after this account, John was seized by Herod the King and cast into prison. As the reality set in that he was never going be released from Herod's dungeon, and perhaps sensing his eventual execution, fear and doubt began to cloud that once unshakable faith. John knew that Christ must increase, and he must decrease (John 3:30), but he was now beginning to understand exactly what that entailed.

From prison, John sent messengers to Jesus asking him if He is really the long-awaited Messiah or should we expect someone else (Matthew 11:2–3). Fear had highjacked John's mind, causing all manner of doubts. Like Peter, John was focusing on the "wind and the waves" of his dire circumstances and was starting to sink.

To this request, Jesus gives evidence of His true identity to take back to John. Jesus knew for John to have his confidence and assurance restored; his doubts must be removed. Therefore, Jesus refocused John's mind on truth, as opposed to his circumstances.

> And Jesus answered them, "Go and tell John what you hear and see: the blind receive their sight and the lame walk, lepers are cleansed and the deaf hear, and the dead are raised up, and the poor have good news preached to them. And blessed is the one who is not offended by me." (Matthew 11:4–6)

Like John's fear-induced doubts, some people's struggle with assurance are episodic. They can go long periods of time with relatively little doubt regarding the reality of their salvation. However, when some stressful crisis occurs in their life, the old fears can resurface. There are no overt sins or negligence to attribute the reemergence of their worries. As has been shown in the life of John, the emotion of fear can be the cause of such doubts.

Thus, believers amid an unexpected re-emergence of doubts concerning their salvation should consider if such doubts are being caused by fear of some new stress or change in their life. This certainly was the case in my own life. Major life challenges and/ or changes were often accompanied by new seasons of doubt concerning my salvation. I will say more about why such doubt may occur in stressful situations in the following chapter, but for now simply try to determine if you can identify such a connection with your own struggles with assurance.

Fear's ability to cause doubt is extremely important to recognize if you struggle with obsessive compulsive disorder. In fact, OCD is often referred to as the "doubting disorder." People who suffer with OCD often doubt their own logic, intelligence, and even intentions. Though, this had been a known characteristic of the disorder, recent studies are now focusing on the devastating role doubt plays in the lives of individuals with OCD.

The first to conduct a clinical study on the role of doubt in OCD was Gerald Nestadt, professor of psychiatry and behavioral sciences at Johns Hopkins. Nestadt and his colleagues reported an investigation of 1,182 adults with OCD who were assessed to eval-uate the relationship between doubt and OCD's clinical features.[41]

The study found that doubt in patients with OCD was strongly related to the number of checking symptoms (compulsions). Nestadt's study also proved that the more doubtful a person is, the more dys-functional they are.

Those who doubt their salvation, and who also have OCD, will most likely have more difficulty attaining and maintaining assurance. However, it is not impossible or even unlikely for them to attain assurance; individuals with OCD just have one more obstacle to overcome than those who are unaffected by the disorder.

Fear causes distraction: The Exodus generation

If fear's ability to cause doubt is not mastered, it may lead to the more powerful delusion of distraction. This too, is a recognized phenomenon in both the Scriptures and psychology. When we doubt our own ability or God's empowerment to face great challenges we may distract our minds from these stressful realities, by imagining something more terrifying that has no basis in truth. A classic exam-ple of this can be found in the book of Numbers.

After being delivered from bondage in Egypt, the children of Israel were very afraid to enter the land of Canaan. The promised land was inhabited by fierce nations who lived in fortified cities. In addition, the Sons of Anak (giants) were living in the land.

To distract themselves by such fearful adversaries, the Israelites imagined something even more frightening—that God was secretly plotting to kill them! Instead of admitting their own fear and asking God to strengthen their hands, they lied against the truth (James 3:14) and maligned the character of God in the process.

---

[41] G. Nestadt, V. Kamath, B. S. Maher, J. Krasnow, P. Nestadt, Y. Wang, A. Bakker, J. Samuels. "Doubt and the Decision-Making Process in Obsessive-Compulsive Disorder." *Med Hypotheses*; 96 (November, 2016):1–4. doi: 10.1016/j.mehy.2016.09.010; Epub September 20, 2016; PMID: 27959266; PMCID: PMC6013040.

Then all the congregation raised a loud cry, and the people wept that night. And all the people of Israel grumbled against Moses and Aaron. The whole congregation said to them, "Would that we had died in the land of Egypt! Or would that we had died in this wilderness! Why is the LORD bringing us into this land, to fall by the sword? Our wives and our little ones will become a prey. Would it not be better for us to go back to Egypt?" (Numbers 14:1–3)

God had demonstrated His love by delivering the Israelites with a mighty hand from Egypt, a nation much more powerful than any they would face in Canaan. Moreover, God protected them from the ravages of the plagues, as well as from the destroyer, a being of immense power sent to kill the first born of Egypt. No other generation in Israel's history had seen such miraculous salvation on their behalf as that generation witnessed. However, because of the distracting power of fear they concluded it was all done to have them slaughtered in the wilderness.

Yet the Jews of the Exodus were not the only example in Scripture that illustrates fear's distracting ability on the mind. Solomon observed that a lazy, worthless person can scare himself into a frenzy just to avoid his responsibilities. Christ noted this same phenomenon in His parable of the talents.

The sluggard says, "There is a lion in the road! There is a lion in the streets!" (Proverbs 26:13)

"Master, I knew you to be a hard man, reaping where you did not sow, and gathering where you scattered no seed, so I was afraid, and I went and hid your talent in the ground. Here, you have what is yours." But his master answered him, "You wicked and slothful servant! You knew

128

that I reap where I have not sown and gather where I scattered no seed? Then you ought to have invested my money with the bankers, and at my coming I should have received what was my own with interest." (Matthew 25:24b-27)

Fear's use as a distraction is not a phenomenon observed solely in the faithless, slothful, or wicked, nor is the accompanying slander and accusation always directed at God or someone else. Oftentimes good God-fearing people when faced with some frightening reality, will direct their distracting fear inward. Remember the apostles one by one each asking Jesus if they were the ones who would betray Him (Matthew 26:22)? As Spurgeon observes, "It is a beautiful trait in the character of the disciples that they did not suspect one another, but *every one of them* inquired, almost incredulously, as the form of the question implies, '*Lord, is it I?*' No one said, 'Lord is it Judas?'"

It is noble to see the Judas within before we see the Judas without: However, like fear's propensity to cause doubt, if fear's ability to cause distraction is not mastered it can become pathologic. This is also a well-documented and studied phenomenon in psychology. Consider this case study from Lucinda Bassett, author of the best-selling book *From Panic to Power.*

When Arty arrived at the Midwest Center, he'd say I don't know what's wrong with me, but the day before I leave to come to the group, I start having these horrible thoughts of hurting myself. Then, every time I get on that bridge, I start thinking about hurting my children. I adore my children. I know I would never hurt them. So why do I have these thoughts? It was obvious. He was so afraid of being out of control on the bridge, he distracted himself with the most terrible thoughts he could dream up: hurting his children. It worked. The thoughts were so horrifying they effectively took his mind off the real problem: being on a bridge with no way out.[42]

Modern psychiatry explains Arty's distracting symptoms as, "unwanted intrusive thoughts." These are distressing and frightening thoughts that enter one's mind and can become "stuck"; ironically from the mental effort exerted to banish them. I already shared in chapter 3 how Hebb's law explains the physiology of this process. This phenomenon, called the "ironic process of the mind," is classically illustrated in a simple experiment.

Subjects are instructed not to think about a certain object for two minutes. They must record each time they do think about it. The experiment is repeated next for four minutes. This time if they think about the object, they must restart the four-minute time-period. Most study participants quit in exasperation! Invariably the more effort that is expended to not think about the forbidden object, the more likely the person will do so. Winston and Seif explain:

> The simple truth is what you resist tends to persist. This is the basic paradox—the ironic process—at work in making unwanted intrusive thoughts so persistent. Thoughts stick because of the energy you expend to fight them.[43]

What makes this matter more distressing is the distracting thoughts that are especially repugnant are the ones that get struggled against the most and as a result tend to get firmly ensconced in the brain. Therefore, psychiatrists refer to such thoughts as, "*egodystonic*," meaning they are always the exact opposite of the true nature of the individual. This is why blasphemous thoughts are most common for

---

[42] Lucinda Bassett, *From Panic to Power* (New York; Harper Collins Publishers, 1996), 82.

[43] Sally Winston and Martin Seif, *Overcoming Unwanted Intrusive Thoughts* (Oakland; New Harbinger Publications, 2017), 14.

genuine believers who suffer from intrusive thoughts. Again, Bunyan is a prime example.

> For, about the space of a month after, a very great storm came down upon me, which handled me twenty times worse than all I had met with before; it came stealing upon me, now by one piece, then by another: First, all my comfort was taken from me; then darkness seized upon me; after which, whole floods of blasphemies, both against God, Christ, and the scriptures, were poured upon my spirit, to my great confusion and astonishment.[44]

Modern descriptions of intrusive thoughts, a common symptom of obsessive-compulsive disorder, such as Arty's and Bunyan's, perhaps point to what the divines described as, *"sudden vehement temptations."* You will recall that the WCF identified such temptations as one of six reasons for a lack of assurance. Note how Bunyan describes these thoughts, *"suddenly"*; *"stealing upon me"*; *"floods of blasphemies,"* etc.

There is a related phenomenon to intrusive thoughts called "thought-action fusion," which makes such thoughts even more distressing. Osborn explains.

> "Thought-action fusion" refers to a tendency to believe that what is depicted in a thought is happening in reality. For example, a person may suddenly have the idea that a loved one has been in an accident. If thought-action fusion take place, he or she will be drawn to believe that the accident has actually occurred, in

---

[44] Ibid., 14,44.

spite of there being no factual basis for drawing that conclusion.[45]

Intrusive thoughts, sudden vehement temptations, thought-action fusion—all are examples of how the emotion of fear can distract a person from facing stressful realities in their life. It has already been stated that not all who doubt their salvation deal with symptoms such as these or have an undiagnosed mental disorder. However, it is highly likely that some do. The good news is these symptoms are well understood now, and highly treatable with cognitive and/or exposure therapy, as well as pharmaceutical correction of brain neurotransmission. Though I will not address specific medical treatment or counseling modalities, it is important to acknowledge their availability and efficacy.

To review, it has been shown that fear in and of itself is not sinful but can lead us into sin when any temporal fear exceeds the fear of God and/ or prevents us from obeying His commands. We also observed, that fear's power to lead us into sin, is made possible by its ability to cause doubt, distraction, and to devolve into other destructive emotions.

We have just looked at two examples from Scripture of fear's effectual leading into sin by causing doubt and distraction. John the Baptist won his battle with doubt and died as he lived—a hero of the faith. Unfortunately, the Exodus generation succumbed to fear's ability to cause distraction, and, as a result, spent the remainder of their lives wandering in the desert.

We will now turn our attention to perhaps fear's most formidable weapon, its ability to devolve into a host of negative and toxic emotions. As with fear's other abilities, that is, to cause doubt and/ or distraction, we will examine two biblical examples. One where fear's capacity for morphing into destructive emotions was managed successfully, as well as an example where it was not. Discussion will begin with a group of believers who lost their battle with fear, being devoured by the anger, hatred and unforgiveness it spawned.

---

[45] Ibid., 152–153.

Fear causes devolution: The Ephesian Church

Most scholars agree that the book of 1 John was written to the Ephesian church in response to the threat of Gnosticism which had begun to impact the church causing confusion, division, and a widespread loss of assurance (1 John 5:13). No doubt people who were perceived to be leaders, or secretly coveted that role, became deceived by this heresy. Not content to simply leave the church, they soon began a campaign to corrupt others. In fact, Paul predicted that this would happen years before (Acts 20:28–31). The authority and doctrine of apostolic teaching was being undermined, and the sheep were being scattered. Fear and panic were the result.

The entire epistle of 1 John was written to bolster the faith of those struggling with assurance (1 John 5:13), and it's noteworthy that John identifies the emotion of fear as the primary cause for those struggles (1 John 4:18). As mentioned, the turmoil within the church caused by the Gnostic heretics had surfaced a host of troubling fears. The doctrines they once knew to be true, were now being brought into question, as was the character of their impeccable teachers; Paul, Timothy, and John. As the psalmist says, "If the foundations be destroyed, what can the righteous do?" (Psalm 11:3).

Interestingly, the environment of doctrinal upheaval in the Ephesian church was strikingly similar to the circumstances during the Renaissance, which also saw significant changes of influence and control within the church. Osborn notes that medical historians who study the period report that, "the number of mentally ill reached alarming proportions," causing entire "epidemics of psychopathies." Cases of scrupulosity, blasphemous intrusive thoughts, melancholy and even anorexia nervosa were all reported in an alarming percentage of the population during this time period.[46]

History has a way of repeating itself, and predictably the global disorder caused by the COVID-19 pandemic has also manifested a similar outbreak of obsessional fears. In his interview with Time,

---

[46] Ibid., 34–44.

Dr. Andrew Guzick, clinical psychologist at the Baylor College of Medicine, confirms as much.

> "Studies have consistently shown that people without OCD have scored higher on our OCD assessments than they did before the pandemic… They are exhibiting more OCD-like behaviors and reporting more intrusive fears characteristic of OCD."[47]

As Guzick noted, there have been a host of studies showing the link between new cases of OCD and exacerbation of existing ones because of the concerns associated with COVID-19. Therefore, it is worth asking yourself, Have your struggles with assurance increased during the COVID-19 pandemic? If so, perhaps your recent struggles with assurance are merely a distraction from facing the fears associated with the virus.

Returning our attention to the Ephesians, it is impossible to determine if the fear they experienced manifested in symptoms like that experienced during the Renaissance and the COVID-19 pandemic. However, it is highly likely some did. Regardless, John stresses that the perfect love of God is the remedy to that fear.

> There is no fear in love, but perfect love casts out fear. For fear has to do with punishment, and whoever fears has not been perfected in love. (1 John 4:18)

Additionally, John explains that the love of God is perfected by two things: persistent obedience to God and demonstrations of love to others. Remember, this is exactly what Peter taught in his sorites in

---

[47] Jeffrey Kluger, "Pandemic Anxiety Is Fueling OCD Symptoms—Even for People Without the Disorder" (*Time*, January, 2022).

2 Peter 1:5–8 discussed in the previous chapter. Below are the verses from 1 John showing exactly how the love of God is perfected.

> But whoever keeps his word, in him truly the love of God is perfected. (1 John 2:5a)

> If we love one another, God abides in us and his love is perfected in us. (1 John 4:12b)

> God is love, and whoever abides in love abides in God, and God abides in him. By this is love perfected with us. (1 John 4 16b-17a)

In response to the Gnostic heretics, the Ephesians circled their wagons as it were and focused solely on the internal graces Peter said we are to add to our faith (virtue, knowledge, self-control, steadfastness, and godliness) stopping short of brotherly affection and love. However, fear was their real enemy, and love was necessary for their victory over it.

Unfortunately, this seed of fear evidently took root and grew. In John's final correspondence to the Ephesian church, he records Jesus' own estimation of the state of their local body.

> To the angel of the church in Ephesus write: "The words of him who holds the seven stars in his right hand, who walks among the seven golden lampstands."
>
> "I know your works, your toil and your patient endurance, and how you cannot bear with those who are evil, but have tested those who call themselves apostles and are not, and found them to be false.
>
> "I know you are enduring patiently and bearing up for my name's sake, and you have not grown weary.

"But I have this against you, that you have abandoned the love you had at first.

"Remember therefore from where you have fallen; repent, and do the works you did at first. If not, I will come to you and remove your lampstand from its place, unless you repent." (Rev. 2:1–5)

Unlike the negligence and/or disobedience that characterizes the obstacle to assurance, *uncommitted in walk*, the Ephesians' actions were evident, praiseworthy in fact. Consider how well they started with regards to Peter's list of the seven graces necessary for assurance.

1. They exhibited *"virtue" ("I know your works")*.
2. They were discerning in their *"knowledge" ("tested those who call themselves apostles")*.
3. They exercised *"self-control" ("your toil")*.
4. They remained consistent in their *"steadfastness" ("your patient endurance")*.
5. They were zealous in their *"godliness" ("bearing up for my namesake")*.

The Ephesians nailed the first five graces on Peter's list, and Christ praised them for it. However, they were so focused on cleansing from their ranks every person and doctrine that deviated from orthodoxy that they stopped short of adding *brotherly affection* and *love ("you have abandoned the love you had at first")*. Steve Gregg offers further insight on the Ephesian abandonment of their first love.

> Though the Christians had not become weary in well doing, they had become negligent in the most important area: you have left your first love (v. 4). Whether the love of God or one another is intended is not specified, though the two likely are not to be sharply differentiated (John 13:34; 1 John 4:20). The loss of love is no

minor defect, but constitutes a fallen state of the church, requiring that they repent and do the first works (v. 5) if they are to avoid the threatened judgment.[48]

The Ephesians did not heed John's first warning that fear must be cast out by both obedience and love. Similarly, people who struggle with assurance often will hyper-focus on doing all the things they believe are godly. Their motives are genuine, and efforts are commendable. For a season, their minds are soothed by the balm of good works, but deep down their lack of assurance remains. The fear is only dormant. Their struggles will invariably return alongside some new stressful event that overwhelms them and exposes the absence of love. Christ knew this would eventually happen to the Ephesians and called them to be restored in love.

The real enemy of the Ephesian church was fear. That fear devolved into anger, hatred and unforgiveness and consumed them. Sadly, the emotion of fear proved too powerful for them, and before the close of the second century, the once great Ephesian church ceased to exist, it's lampstand was removed.

Fear causes devolution: David the King

As Dr. Kubler-Ross noted, fear will undoubtedly lead to other negative emotions. We have already seen how the destructive emotions of anger and hatred spawned by fear robbed the Ephesians of their assurance and ultimately destroyed the entire church.

Feelings of guilt and shame also arise from fear, and often play a significant role in people who have lost their assurance. Therefore, it is necessary to clearly define each of these emotions and go into greater detail regarding their role in the development of the spiritual stronghold of assurance-doubt.

---

[48] Steve Gregg, *Revelation Four Views, A Parallel Commentary* (Nashville; Thomas Nelson Publishers, 1997), 65.

Though the emotions of guilt and shame are often used inter-changeably, there is a significant difference between the two. Clinical psychologist Dr. Joseph Burgo provides a clear distinction.

> Guilt and shame sometimes go hand in hand; the same action may give rise to feelings of both shame and guilt, where the former reflects how we feel about ourselves and the latter involves an awareness that our actions have injured some-one else. In other words, shame relates to self; guilt to others.[49]

According to Burgo, guilt is the emotion we feel when we become aware of how our actions hurt another person, whereas shame is the emotion we feel when we realize what our hurtful behavior reveals about our own character. Both emotions will become toxic and wreck our assurance if left unaddressed in a biblical manner.

People weighed down by the burden of guilt and shame may say, "I know in my head that God loves me, but I don't feel it in my heart," or "I know the Bible says I can't lose my salvation, but maybe I'm the exception"? Comments such as these point to an emotional block that needs removed, a wound that needs to be healed, sins that to be need confessed and forgiven.

Working through the guilt and shame felt from one's sinful past is a process. It's length and intensity depend on several factors. The particulars of the causative sin and the severity of its consequences influence the process. The psychological make-up of the person involved, and the effectiveness of his or her support network (i.e., family, friends, church, etc.), also play an important role.

The process of restoration from the consequences of guilt and shame has specific steps. Each must be walked through. There are no short cuts. The journey requires courage, honesty, and humility.

---

[49] Joseph Burgo, The Difference Between Guilt and Shame (Psychology Today, 2023 Sussex Publishers, LLC) May 30, 2013.

King David successfully went through this process, and the details of his journey, provide the blueprint for genuine restoration.

Most are familiar with the tragic circumstances of David's adultery with Bathsheba, and subsequent murder of her husband, Uriah the Hittite. For nearly a year David tried to hide from and cover up his sins. Later in his life, David reflected on the physical and emotional toll this grim period had on him.

> For when I kept silent, my bones wasted away through my groaning all day long.
> For day and night your hand was heavy upon me; my strength was dried up as by the heat of summer. Selah (Psalm 32:3–4)

After finally having his grievous sins exposed by Nathan, the prophet, David released all the guilt and shame he had been carrying for nearly a year, and in the process, he provides a picture for genuine repentance and restoration. David's cathartic encounter with God is found in Psalm 51, which the Lutheran Reformer, Victorinus Strigelius described as "the brightest gem in the whole book, and contains instruction so large, and doctrine so precious, that the tongue of angels could not do justice to the full development." It is in this powerful psalm of David that the following steps in the process of restoration can be found.

1. Confession and repentance
2. Mourning and grieving our sin
3. Separating forgiveness from consequences
4. Healing through the body

1. Confession and repentance

This process may seem like a daunting task, but the good news is from God's perspective, only the first step is necessary, confession and repentance. Genuine biblical confession is the full and accurate acknowledgment of one's sin. It includes both vertical (1 John

1:9) and horizontal (James 5:16) components. David, the man after God's own heart, exemplifies the distinct marks of true confession and repentance which will be discussed next.

a. *Assigning our sin.*

The first mark of true confession and repentance is assigning correct ownership of sin. There is no room for excuse making, blame shifting or rationalization. No doubt David spent an agonizing year doing all three. One can imagine some of David's tormented thoughts: "If Bathsheba wasn't bathing on her roof top this never would have happened," "God, why didn't You stop me as when You sent Abigail to prevent me from killing Nabal?" "For the sake of peace and stability of the nation, it's better that one man should die." Of course, these musings of David are speculative, but human nature, such as it is, makes these rationalizations or those like them very probable. Regardless, David was done with such disingenuous behavior. He was finally ready to assign the guilt where it belongs—"*my transgressions*," "*my sins*," and "*my iniquity*"—and he does so immediately in the first three verses.

1) Have mercy on me, O God,
according to your steadfast love;
according to your abundant mercy
blot out my transgressions.
2) Wash me thoroughly from my iniquity,
and cleanse me from my sin!
3) For I know my transgressions,
and my sin is ever before me. (Psalm 51:1–3)

b. *Acknowledging that sin is against God.*

The second step for genuine confession is acknowledging that sin is ultimately against God. David is not dismissing the terrible sins he committed against Bathsheba and Uriah for the guilt and shame he felt. Yet he recognized that his rebellion, rejection, and despising of God and His Word, as the wicked seed that sprouted to such an evil act (James 1:15).

> 4) Against you, you only, have I sinned
>   and done what is evil in your sight,
>   so that you may be justified in your
>   words
>   and blameless in your judgment.
>   (Psalm 51:4)

c. *Accepting your own depravity.*

MENE MENE TEKEL UPHARSIN—these are the foreboding words written by a ghostly hand to Belshazzar, the self-indulgent and degenerate grandson of Nebuchadnezzar and heir to the throne of Babylon (Daniel 5:27). From this ancient prophecy we get the modern expressions "the handwriting is on the wall" and "your days are numbered." Daniel interpreted the cryptic message: MENE MENE ("your days are numbered"), TEKEL ("you have been weighed in the balances and found wanting"), and UPHARSIN ("your kingdom is divided and given to the Medes and Persians"). That very night Babylon fell, and Darius the Mede executed Belshazzar.

It's a tough thing to be, "*weighed in the balances and found wanting*" (Daniel 5:27). It's especially tough when you have a history of significant accomplishments, and are held in high esteem by others, as was the case with David. Nevertheless, accepting your own depravity; is the third step that must be taken in biblical confession.

David understood his fallen nature intellectually, but now he was experiencing it, feeling it. Centuries later, Elijah (1 Kings 19:4) and Peter (Matthew 26:75) would have to walk through that same valley of shame on their journey to restoration. It is extremely difficult and disillusioning when we realize just how wretched we really are.

However, without that acceptance and determination to genuinely repent, our shame and guilt will cling to us in a cloak of bitterness.

> 5) Behold, I was brought forth in iniquity,
> and in sin did my mother conceive
> me. (Psalm 51:5)

d. Avoiding disingenuous repentance.

It is interesting to see how various animals transfer leadership from one dominant individual to another. Most of the time the transfer of power is peaceful however sometimes it can be brutal, even deadly. For example, when a young bull hippo challenges the current alpha male, the fight is extremely fierce. If the younger bull gains the upper hand, the first thing he does is bite off the tail of his opponent. Next, the former leader is chased away from the herd until he is out of his old territory. However, the old bull is still a formidable threat, and control is very hard to let go of. Therefore, the young bull will continue the pursuit until the former alpha male lies prostrate on his belly in submission to the new leader.

This example from the animal kingdom illustrates the final step in biblical confession, avoiding insincere repentance. God is not as ruthless as the young hippo, but he is as persistent. For our own good He will not allow us to persist in hypocritical or disingenuous repentance.

There are two Greek words used in the New Testament for repentance. The verb metamelomai, denotes "a change of mind, such as to produce regret or even remorse on account of sin, but not necessarily a change of heart." This word is used with reference to the repentance of Judas after his betrayal of Christ (Matthew 27:3). This type of repentance is tantamount to the old hippo coming back to reclaim his territory. The second Greek word is *metanoeo*. It refers to a change of one's mind and purpose. This verb, with the cognate noun *metanoia*, is used of true repentance, a change of mind and purpose in life, to which remission of sin is promised.

A true sense of one's own guilt and sinfulness is required for genuine repentance, as is a determined effort to live a holy life (Psalm 51:13). David had both. Believers struggling with assurance due to guilt and shame must honestly assess whether they have met all the conditions necessary for genuine confession and repentance from past sins.

2.   Mourning and grieving

The Puritans used to pray for the; "gift of tears." They understood that genuine repentance was ultimately a gift from God (Acts 11:18). The Puritans also knew what Jesus meant when He said, "Happy are those who mourn for they will be comforted" (Matthew 5:4). The comfort of course is forgiveness, and the release of emotions as we mourn and grieve our sin is an important part of that comfort.

Nobody would argue that David was not genuinely forgiven and repentant. In fact, the first thing Nathan said to David after his confession was, "The Lord has put away your sin; you shall not die," (2 Samuel 12:13). David's own gut-wrenching confession in the first few verses of Psalm 51, and his pledge of obedience in later verses, prove the genuineness of his repentance. Yet he still was in need for God to restore unto him the joy of his salvation. David knew in his head that he was forgiven, but he didn't feel it yet. *"Purge me," "Wash me"; "Cast me not away," "Don't take your Holy Spirit away from me,"* are heartfelt expressions of a man still feeling the effects of the guilt and shame of his actions.

> 6)   Purge me with hyssop, and I shall be clean;
> wash me, and I shall be whiter than snow.
> 7)   Let me hear joy and gladness;

143

let the bones that you have broken
rejoice.

8) Hide your face from my sins,
   and blot out all my iniquities.
9) Create in me a clean heart, O God,
   and renew a right spirit within me.
10) Cast me not away from your presence,
    and take not your Holy Spirit from
    me.
11) Restore to me the joy of your salvation,
    and uphold me with a willing spirit.
    (Psalm 51:7–12)

People struggling with assurance due to shame and guilt perhaps have never fully expressed their own sorrow over past sins and
failings. This is a step that cannot be dismissed. Grief over our sins
will lead to another important reality we must mourn. Namely, the
death of the man or woman we thought we were.

After Peter's betrayal of Christ, the Bible says that he wept bit-
terly. Jesus predicted Peter's betrayal but also assured him that after
he mourned his sin he would return to a position of leadership (Luke
22:32). Similarly, after Elijah fled from Jezibel, he too confessed, "It
is enough O Lord, take my life, for I am no better than my fathers" (1
Kings 19:4). Like Peter, Elijah was also restored to his ministry after
his own period of mourning (1 Kings 19:15–18). This painful emotional path both men experienced was necessary for their restoration
and return to service.

"MENE MENE TEKEL UPHARSIN." It is indeed a tough
thing to be weighed in the balances and found wanting. Perhaps this
is partly why Paul says not to think more highly of ourselves than we
ought to think (Romans 12:3). It makes the fall that much steeper,
and painful.

3. Separating forgiveness and consequences

The forgiveness of God is independent from the consequences of sin or the guilt and remorse we inevitably feel as a result. This is a critical concept for people struggling with assurance of salvation to grasp, especially those who also have OCD.

Because of the way the brain works in people with OCD, they may mull and obsess over past failures much longer than those who are unaffected by the disorder. Even after we have mourned and grieved over our sin, the consequences may remain. In some situations, the consequences of sin are severe and permanent. Dealing with such consequences can cause periodic episodes of grief and remorse. One cannot equate that grief with the false idea that God has forsaken them. They must also expect Satan, the great accuser of the brethren (Revelation 12:10), to seize on such moments of regret.

Nathan outlined the consequences for his sin that David would have to face (2 Samuel 12:10–14). Undoubtedly those consequences were echoing in David's mind as he repeatedly asked God to cleanse him. Yet David gained the ability to separate the gracious reality of his forgiveness from the tragic consequences of his sin (2 Samuel 12:23).

Samson, the strongest man who ever lived, never got his eyesight back. Moses, the great law giver, was not allowed to enter the Holy Land. David, Israel's greatest king and a man after God's own heart, lost his child and reaped a lifetime of horrific consequences. However, each of these three men are listed in the book of Hebrews, as great heroes of the faith. This realization should provide much comfort for those yet working through the separation of forgiveness and consequences.

4. Healing through the body

As stated earlier, there is a vertical (1 John 1:9) and horizontal (James 5:16) aspect to confession. Each has its own purpose. John explains that confessing our sins to God provides forgiveness and cleansing, while James says that confessing our sins to each other brings about healing and closure. Drs. Henry Cloud and John Townsend provide keen insight on the different purposes of each.

> While the head works with "information gathering," the heart works with "experience gathering." This is one of the meanings behind James 5:16, which says, "Therefore confess your sins to each other and pray for each other so that you may be healed." Many Christians do the vertical confession of 1 John 1:9, where they confess to God, but not to others. So they "know" they are forgiven and loved in their head, they just don't "know" it in their heart. We are made to experience both, and it is one of the reasons that Jesus commands us to love one another.[50]

In his book *The Art of Forgiveness, Lovingkindness and Peace*, Jack Kornfield describes an African forgiveness ritual that wonderfully captures the essence of the healing and closure that James refers to.

> In the Babemba tribe of South Africa, when a person acts irresponsibly or unjustly, he is placed in the center of the village, alone and unfettered. All work ceases, and every man, woman, and child in the village gathers in a large circle around the accused individual. Then each person in the tribe speaks to the accused, one at a time, each recalling the good things the person in the center of the circle has done in his lifetime. Every incident, every experience that can be recalled with any detail and accuracy, is recounted. All his positive attributes, good deeds, strengths, and kind-

---

[50] Henry Cloud and John Townsend, *How People Grow* (Grand Rapids; Zondervan, 2001), 128.

nesses are recited carefully and at length. This tribal ceremony often lasts for several days. At the end, the tribal circle is broken, a joyous celebration takes place, and the person is symbolically and literally welcomed back into the tribe.[51]

This beautiful ritual powerfully illustrates why some people can walk through each of the steps of confession and repentance, and still have little emotional closure. They have owned their sin and accepted the consequences. Yet something is missing. Unfortunately for people with assurance struggles, this burden can become another piece of evidence in the case against them. They need to complete this final step. They need healing through the body of Christ.

Final thoughts

In summary, it has been shown how our emotions can be the causative force for struggles with assurance. The sinful response to the emotion of fear is particularly implicated in the initial development of the spiritual stronghold of assurance-doubt, and the negative secondary emotions spawned from fear keep the stronghold intact.

We saw from the example of John the Baptist how fear can cause us to doubt the things we know to be true, including our salvation. Fear can also play tricks on the mind as a distraction from facing fearful or unpleasant realities, as was the case with the Exodus generation. Similarly, instead of dealing with their real problems or fears head on, some people will distract their minds with a wide variety of frightening "what-if?" doubts regarding their salvation.

Not only can fear cause doubt and distraction, but fear also gives rise to other destructive emotions that can be the source of persistent struggles with assurance. We saw from the Ephesian church how fear caused by the Gnostic heretics not only caused them to lose their assurance, but also led to anger and hatred which prevented them

---

[51] Jack Kornfield, *The Art of Forgiveness, Lovingkindness and Peace* (London; Bantom, 2008), 42.

from regaining it. After David committed adultery with Bathsheba and had her husband, Uriah, murdered, he also was filled with the fear of blood guilt punishment (Psalm 51:14; 2 Samuel 12:13). When Nathan assured David that he was forgiven and would not die, that initial fear was removed allowing the guilt and shame to surface. Despite being assured of his forgiveness, it was impossible for David to experience the assurance of his salvation until he dealt completely with his guilt and shame.

The biblical examples of David, the Ephesians, John the Baptist, and the Exodus generation demonstrate how fear and the negative emotions it spawns can be the major source for our struggles with assurance. Jesus refocused John's mind on truth to dispel his fear and doubt, enabling John to face his end with the same confident assurance he had when he began his ministry to "prepare the way of LORD; and make his paths straight" (Matthew 3:3). David also successfully dealt with his guilt and shame, averting a lifetime of bitterness and regret, having the joy of his salvation restored.

However, the Ephesians were never corporately restored as a local body. The fear and panic inflicted upon them by the Gnostic heretics; became a permanent state of anger, hatred, and unforgiveness. The Exodus generation was also unsuccessful in managing fear's ability to cause distraction; and, as a result, never stepped one foot in the promised land. Neither group were able to conquer their specific battle with fear, thus failing to overcome the obstacle of *unrestored in emotions*.

Let the ancient Israelites and the Ephesians be a warning for you in your efforts to overcome this obstacle. Until you win the battle with fear and other negative emotions and are restored emotionally, lingering doubts concerning your salvation will remain (see TEA graph).

We have seen in the previous chapter and in this chapter how our actions and emotions can be the impetus for the development of the spiritual stronghold of assurance-doubt. The next two obstacles, *unbiblical in foundation* and *undisciplined in mind* each address the initiating role of our thoughts for struggles with assurance. However, before beginning the next chapter, review the final TEA graph for the obstacle *unrestored in emotions* and ask the Holy Spirit to help you answer the "Mindful Question" as thoroughly and honestly as possible.

Mindful question

Consider the examples of the Ephesians and David. Are you harboring any bitterness and unforgiveness for those who have harmed you in the past? Are you still plagued by regret and remorse from past sins?

9

GAME PLAN–PHASE 4: IMPLEMENTATION

Gentlemen, this is a football.

—Vince Lombardi

I began discussion of the implementation phase for our game plan for attaining the assurance of salvation by addressing the importance of our actions. From there, the causal role our emotions play in assurance-doubt was examined. You'll recall that I advised to progress through each chapter of this book in order and not to skip ahead. This is especially true regarding these chapters that address the implementation of the five key obstacles to the assurance of salvation. By beginning with our actions and then addressing our emotions, we are slowly "peeling back the onion" to get to the foundational core for most struggles with assurance, our thoughts (see TEA graph below). It is worth noting that the WCF also listed their reasons for assurance-doubt in this exact order, beginning with actions, then emotions, and finally thoughts.

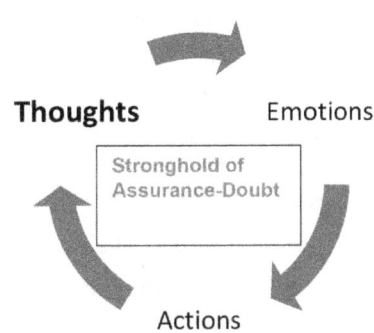

Formation of assurance-doubt stronghold initiated by our thoughts.

Thoughts   Emotions

Stronghold of Assurance-Doubt

Actions

Vince Lombardi, the Hall of Fame coach of the Green Bay Packers once began training camp by stressing the importance of laying a proper foundation in a rather facetious manner. "Gentlemen, this is a football. If somebody throws it to you, catch it. If somebody hands it to you, run with it. If you see it lying on the ground, pounce on it. Your careers depend on what you do with this football"!

All football coaches recognize the importance of the fundamentals of the sport and the impact they have on the success or failure of the team. Invariably at some point during the season, failure of implementing the fundamentals of the game becomes woefully apparent. The blocking and tackling starts to get sloppy, the routes run by the receivers aren't as crisp, and the basic reads of the QB are not executed. As a result, the overall offensive and defensive performance begins to break down.

At this deteriorating point of the season, some coaches waste valuable time questioning their schemes and search for some "magical" playlist that may be the answer to their problems. However, the experienced coaches go back to the foundation and refocus their team on executing the fundamentals of the game.

The team always returns to a high level of performance once they are reestablished in the fundamentals. Also, these "back to the basics" points in the season often exposes critical gaps in a few player's understanding of the fundamentals. For such players, exponential growth is often seen in their performance after they finally master the elementary techniques of their position.

Assurance Fundamentals: Understanding the Scriptures and Self

Similarly, people struggling with assurance must also go back to the fundamentals and examine their understanding of two separate foundational topics. The first topic is the fundamental teaching of Scripture regarding the promises of salvation and the eternal security of a believer. The second topic is the humble and sober assessment of themselves.

Central to both of these foundational topics, is an accurate estimation of one's fallen nature and the frailties that now characterize each one of us. Like a football player who finally grasps all of the fundamentals of his position, exponential growth in assurance will be achieved when a person fully grasps these two critical topics.

The great Anglican Bishop, J. C. Ryle, coined the phrase, "The best of men are men at best." Nobody knows the truth of that statement more than God. He knows our fallenness and our frailties (Psalm 103:14). A correct understanding of the promises of salvation and the eternal security of the believer is predicated upon the comprehension of the pervasive fallenness of the human condition.

In light of our fallenness, God not only had to save us, but he must keep us saved. Jesus said, "No one can come to me unless the Father who sent me draws him. And I will raise him up on the last day" (John 6:44). This is a remarkable statement by Christ! As fallen human beings, we are incapable of coming to God for salvation of our own accord, let alone keeping our salvation by our own strength.

God must move us to come to Him and preserve us afterwards. Fully comprehending God's exclusive role in salvation and preservation is paramount to assurance. Any contribution from a human standpoint to either salvation or its preservation would only introduce corruption and make both an impossibility. This baseline knowledge is prerequisite to overcoming the obstacle of *unbiblical in foundation*.

I mentioned the second fundamental topic necessary for assurance is a humble and sober evaluation of one's self. In particular, those lacking assurance must understand how deep-seated beliefs held about themselves, and faulty thinking patterns, influence their ability to apprehend or claim the eternal promises of salvation.

As a result of the fall, man is now defined by his frailty which manifests to one degree or another in an aberrant and dysfunctional mind. The distorted beliefs and thoughts now common to the human condition must be mastered by the truth of God to overcome the obstacle of *undisciplined in mind.*

Thus, for assurance to be achieved a person must not only understand the promises of Scripture, but also be able to consciously claim these promises for himself. Therefore, comprehension and apprehension are both necessary for assurance. Both of these requirements occur in the mind, therefore, I chose to address these final two obstacles of assurance in tandem.

Mining all of Scripture to thoroughly grasp a specific doctrine is a daunting task, as is the study required to understand all the psychological underpinnings that influence our thoughts and temperaments. Such an exhaustive approach is beyond the scope and purpose of our game plan. However, the subjects that are addressed, namely the eternal, irrevocable, and unmerited promises of salvation, along with the psychological hurdles that hinder our ability to trust in those promises, will be appropriately developed.

Incorrect beliefs regarding "salvation and self" often serve as the initial impetus for the development of the spiritual stronghold of assurance-doubt. Regarding salvation, we must understand that our fallen nature necessitates God's exclusive role in the provision and preservation of our salvation. With regards to our self-understanding, we must recognize how the frailties that now characterize us, hinder our ability to trust in God's complete salvific work. Both of these errant beliefs concerning "salvation and self" are graciously addressed in the Word of God.

We already noted that God accommodates our fallenness by promising his exclusive role in our salvation and preservation. However, along with these promises, God also graciously explains what happens the moment we believe to accommodate our frailty. God describes salvation in different ways so we can fully grasp it and explains the critical role He plays to further our trust.

In addition to these descriptive explanations of the promises of eternal security, God also provides another accommodation to our frailty. He supplies evidences of his saving presence in our lives that we can test for ourselves. He provides His Holy Spirit to produce these evidences, and His Word to help us consciously recognize them (Galatians 5:22–23; John 16:13; Romans 8:16).

Again because of the necessity of both comprehension and apprehension to attain assurance, the obstacles of *unbiblical in foundation* and *undisciplined in mind* will be discussed in tandem and organized around the two topics listed below.

1. Promises of Salvation and Possessing the Promises
2. Evidences of Salvation and Errors in Thinking

The first topic will discuss the descriptive explanations of salvation that God provides in His Word to aid our comprehension. The second topic will discuss the objective biblical evidences of salvation that once understood, will further buttress our comprehension of salvation. Alongside each topic, I will address the mental hurdles that must be overcome for us to personally apprehend both the promises and evidences of salvation.

1. Promises of salvation and possessing the promises

Promises in pictures

To begin discussion of this first section, it's helpful to use the phenomena of intrusive thoughts and thought-action fusion, discussed earlier as symptoms of obsessive-compulsive disorder as illustrations.

You'll recall that intrusive thoughts, and possibly what the WCF described as "sudden vehement temptations," are those unwanted, disturbing thoughts that pop into our heads without warning, and thought-action fusion is when one believes that simply thinking about an action is equivalent to the actual occurrence of that action. Each of these deceptive brain messages can start the cycle of synergy yielding further negative thoughts, emotions, and compulsions, as Schwartz demonstrates and explains in the following figure.[52]

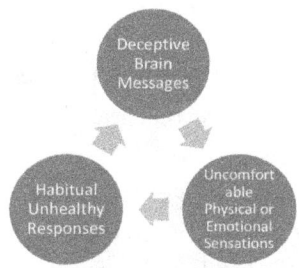

Each time the cycle of; "deceptive brain message→ uncomfortable sensation→ habit → momentary relief" occurs, the underlying brain circuits are strengthened.

However, this same negative synergy that Schwartz describes occurring in OCD can be used for helpful benefits as well. If a desired mental image is positive, memorable, and believable, then it can also be latched on to, yielding constructive benefits instead of destructive. In fact, Paul instructs the Philippians to do just that.

> Finally, brothers, whatever is true, whatever is honorable, whatever is just, whatever is pure, whatever is lovely, whatever is commendable, if there is any excellence, if there is anything worthy of praise, think about these things. What you have learned and received and heard and seen in me—practice these things, and the God of peace will be with you. (Philippians 4:8–9)

Although we looked at this passage earlier, it's helpful to review it again. In this verse Paul instructs the Philippians to meditate on a variety of positive attributes, and to think about how they witnessed these behaviors in his own life. The result of engaging their minds with such thoughts and memories would result in the emotion of peace; and lead to their own godly actions.

---

[52] Ibid., You are Not Your Brain, 75, 81.

I mentioned that for a desired mental image to stick in one's brain, it must be positive and memorable. However, sometimes for a desirable image to thoroughly embed in our minds, it needs to be believable as well. Indeed, vividly noble thoughts that influence us the most are those we deem attainable and thus believable. What helps anything to be attainable and believable is a correct understanding of it. Overcoming the fear of flying is a perfect example to prove this concept.

Research shows that roughly 40 percent of the general population reports some fear of flying, and 2.5 percent to 6 percent have been diagnosed with the clinical phobia, aviophobia.[53] The key to overcoming this fear lies in our understanding of the process of flying, and not our trust in the pilot, no matter how skilled he is, or trying to gin up the courage on our own!

Fear of flying is overcome when a thorough explanation of airplane design and the physics of flying is given. When further education such as the nature of turbulence, safety statistics, etc. is provided, a person's fear of flying often disappears completely.

Just as the guarantee from an ace pilot that "everything will be okay" can fall on deaf ears to someone afraid to fly, so too can the promises of God to people struggling with assurance. Again, God knows our frailties, that we are given to fear and slow to believe and trust. So; He adds to His promise of salvation, beautifully memorable illustrations that explain how and why He alone accomplishes it. These explanations make His promises more understandable. Moreover, since God is the one doing all the work of salvation and preservation, each task is easily attainable and, as a result, more believable.

Jesus used this same teaching style to explain all the facets of the kingdom of heaven and God's tender love for His children. These parables were centered on familiar themes, so they were believable as well as vivid and memorable. One can picture the woman anxiously

---

[53] Sarah Vander Schaaff, "Lots of Americans Have a Fear of Flying. There are Ways to Overcome the Anxiety Disorder." *Washington Post*, October 12, 2019, Health.

sweeping her home searching for her lost coin, or thoroughly kneading yeast in the dough of her bread (Luke 15:8; Matthew 13:33). The excitement of the man finding a treasure hidden in a field can be felt, as can the pain of the father awaiting the return of his wayward son (Matthew 13:44; Luke 15:20).

These parables were crafted in such a way to spur us on to further meditation, allowing continued guidance from the Holy Spirit (John 16:13). Under the inspiration of God, the writers of the New Testament employ the same teaching mode in describing all the facets of our salvation. Though the descriptions of salvation laid out in Scripture are not parables per se, they nonetheless are positive, memorable and believable and have the same effect on us when meditated upon.

God also describes His promises of salvation to us in various ways so we can fully grasp and trust them. He paints vivid pictures that capture our imagination and calms all our fears. Such "pictures" are meant for our meditation. When one reflects on these promises, all the nuances of God's guarantees of eternal security become evident and cherished. Such contemplation often reveals hidden truths within our inmost being (Psalm 51:6), as will become apparent shortly.

What follows, then, are three such pictures of salvation; that wonderfully display the irrevocable eternality of our salvation. Each picture laid out in the Bible also highlights the exclusive role that God plays in granting, securing, and fulfilling our salvation.

A priceless gift

The first portrait of salvation that I will address comes from the Gospel of John. In John's Gospel, believers are described as a precious gift from the Father to the Son. Below are the verses that serve as the colors for this remarkable picture of our salvation. Take a few minutes and carefully examine each of these verses as if it were the first time you ever read them. Try to spot the specific role that the Father and Son play in our salvation as well as the role, if any we play.

1. All that the Father gives me will come to me, and whoever comes to me I will never cast out. (John 6:37)

2. And this is the will of him who sent me, that I should lose nothing of all that he has given me, but raise it up on the last day. (John 6:39)

3. For this is the will of my Father, that everyone who looks on the Son and believes in him should have eternal life, and I will raise him up on the last day." (John 6:40)

4. I give them eternal life, and they will never perish, and no one will snatch them out of my hand. (John 10:28)

5. My Father, who has given them to me, is greater than all, and no one is able to snatch them out of the Father's hand. (John 10:29)

6. Then comes the end, when he delivers the kingdom to God the Father after destroying every rule and every authority and power. (1 Corinthians 15:24)

These are tremendous verses, pregnant with marvelous truths that demand our meditation. They display not only the tender relationship that the Father has with the Son, but also the priceless value placed on us. Did you spot in these passages the complete absence of any responsibility on our part? We are merely the gift that needs accepted by Christ and safely delivered to our heavenly home. To aid in the meditation on the truth and beauty of this picture of our salvation, imagine a conversation between the Father and His Son in eternity past:

> FATHER: Son, I have a special gift that I want to give to You!
>
> JESUS: Thank You, Father!
>
> FATHER: Now, Son, I want You to accept all of them. Their value is beyond measure, for each are made in Our image.
>
> JESUS: Father, I promise I will never drive any of them away.
>
> FATHER: I also want You to protect them My Son. See to it that they all make it home with Us. They cannot complete the journey on their own. Their enemy is too powerful for them, but not for You.
>
> JESUS: I will give them eternal life and guard them with My own hands! As far as their enemy is concerned, I will crush his head and render him powerless. After I destroy every rule, authority, and power I will deliver them back to You, My Father.
>
> FATHER: I know you will Son. I love them too, so I will guard them with My hands as well!

Though I am no playwright, and have taken some liberty with this script, it is nonetheless biblical and true. Writing out the promises of salvation in such a manner is a helpful way to meditate on the wonderful truths that they convey.

We are a priceless gift that God has given to his Son, and all of God's gifts are irrevocable (Romans 11:29). It is Christ's sole responsibility to safely deliver us to our final home because he is the only one equal to the task. As Paul noted, there is no power in the universe that can prevent Jesus from accomplishing this task!

For I am sure that neither death nor life, nor angels nor rulers, nor things present nor things to come, nor powers, nor height nor depth, nor anything else in all creation, will be able to separate us from the love of God in Christ Jesus our Lord (Romans 8:38–39).

A beloved son

Where John uses the picture of a gift to explain the marvelous truths of our salvation, Paul often used the metaphor of a son, and heir through adoption, to explain our status as believers. As he develops this theme, Paul describes the role each member of the Godhead plays. The Father chooses us from the foundation of the world to be adopted sons and heirs through Christ, and the Holy Spirit provides the guarantee of our ultimate redemption. As with the preceding picture of salvation, carefully read each of these verses before continuing.

1. For you did not receive the spirit of slavery to fall back into fear, but you have received the Spirit of adoption as sons, by whom we cry, "Abba! Father!" The Spirit himself bears witness with our spirit that we are children of God, and if children, then heirs—heirs of God and fellow heirs with Christ, provided we suffer with him in order that we may also be glorified with him. (Romans 8:15–17)

2. In him you also, when you heard the word of truth, the gospel of your salvation, and believed in him, were sealed with the promised Holy Spirit, who is the guarantee of our inheritance until we acquire possession of it, to the praise of his glory. (Ephesians 1:13–14)

3. Even as he chose us in him before the foundation of the world, that we should be holy and blameless before him. In love he predestined us for adoption to himself as sons through Jesus Christ, according to the purpose of his will. (Ephesians 1:4–5)

4. For in Christ Jesus you are all sons of God, through faith. (Galatians 3:25).

5. And if you are Christ's, then you are Abraham's offspring, heirs according to promise. (Galatians 3:29)

6. So you are no longer a slave, but a son, and if a son, then an heir through God. (Galatians 4:7)

Similar to John's "gift" theme, there is nothing in Paul's "sonship" theology that requires anything in advance from a believer to become a son, nor does it identify any requirements to remain a son. Indeed, the decision to make us sons of God was made before we were even born (Philippians 4:3). Geisler summarizes Paul's theology on the sonship of the believer and its inevitable consummation in heaven.

> Believers were predestined to be adopted into God's family before the world began. God knew in advance everything we would do, even after we had been saved, including all our sins. Yet there is nothing that can undo an eternal decree of God (Rom. 11:29). Hence, those who are adopted into his family are eternally secure. There is no such thing in Scripture as being unadopted. He adopted us because he wanted us, even though he knew everything about us in

advance. The Holy Spirit is a guarantee of one's ultimate redemption. Hence, to argue that persons can lose their salvation is tantamount to saying that God's guarantee that believers will reach the ultimate day of redemption is not good![54]

Our future in heaven is guaranteed by the seal of the Spirit of God Himself, and that fact was decided from the foundation of the world. Moreover, in the present there is no condemnation (Romans 8:1). It is very comforting for those struggling with assurance to see themselves eternally secure—past, present, and future. This chronological aspect of our salvation is a dominant theme in each picture of salvation, but I will fully develop it alongside discussion of the final picture we will look at next.

A secured lamb

There are no animals mentioned more in the Bible than sheep. The people of God are often identified as sheep in both the Old and New Testaments, and for good reason. Sheep are defenseless creatures, in need of shepherd to protect them from wild animals. The shepherd must also lead them safely to feeding pastures and drinkable water sources.

Sheep are not as strong as other animals. They cannot carry heavy loads. In fact, they would be crushed under such weighty burdens. Yet sheep are highly valued. Indeed, a man's wealth was often equated with the number of sheep he had, and a faithful shepherd would put his life on the line to protect them.

Like sheep, we are highly valued, yet we are also weak and defenseless without Christ's protection (John 10:11). Therefore, Jesus urges us to cast our burdens on Him (Matthew 11:28–30). Christ alone is able and responsible for getting us safely through this life to our final destination; *"I am the door. If anyone enters by me, he*

---

[54] Norman Geisler, *Four Views on Eternal Security*, ed. Matthew Pinson; (Grand Rapids; Zondervan, 2002), 74–75.

will be saved and will go in and out and find pasture." (John 10:9). Indeed, Jesus is the Good Shepherd prophesied by Ezekiel and Isaiah who would come into the world in the fullness of time and give His life for the sheep (Ezekiel 34:23–24; Isaiah 53:6). It is helpful for those who struggle with assurance to see themselves as sheep; to realize their absolute dependence on Christ, the Good Shepherd, to safely manage all the aspects of their salvation.

Meditating on the chronological features of salvation is also critical for those who struggle with assurance. They need to see this, because they are afraid that somehow in the future, they may lose their salvation. Like a soldier suffering from the shellshock of war, they need to understand the war for their salvation is over, the battle is won, and they are safe at home.

God tenderly explains that for all intents and purposes, we're already safe in heaven because He has decreed it so from eternity past (Ephesians 1:4) nor is there any condemnation in the present. The old has passed away, and the new has come. We have already crossed over from death to life. We are already seated in the heavenlies. We already have eternal life. There is no possibility of perishing. It's too late for us to "screw it up"! Take some time to carefully read each of the following verses associated with the "secured lamb" picture of salvation.

1. And I will set up one shepherd over them, and he shall feed them, even my servant David; he shall feed them, and he shall be their shepherd. And I the LORD will be their God, and my servant David a prince among them; I the LORD have spoken it. (Ezekiel 34:23–24)

2. All we like sheep have gone astray; we have turned—every one—to his own way; and the LORD has laid on him the iniquity of us all. (Isaiah 53:6)

3. "I am the door. If anyone enters by me, he will be saved and will go in and out and find pasture." (John 10:9)

4. My sheep hear my voice, and I know them, and they follow me. I give them eternal life, and they will never perish. (John 10:27a)

5. Truly, truly, I say to you, whoever hears my word and believes him who sent me has eternal life. He does not come into judgment, but has passed from death to life. (John 5:24)

6. Before him will be gathered all the nations, and he will separate people one from another as a shepherd separates the sheep from the goats. And he will place the sheep on his right, but the goats on the left. Then the King will say to those on his right, "Come, you who are blessed by my Father, inherit the kingdom prepared for you from the foundation of the world." (Matthew 25:32–34)

7. Therefore, if anyone is in Christ, he is a new creation. The old has passed away; behold, the new has come. (2 Corinthians 5:17)

8. Even as he chose us in him before the foundation of the world, that we should be holy and blameless before him. (Ephesians 1:4a)

9. Even when we were dead in our trespasses, made us alive together with Christ—by grace you have been saved—and raised us

up with him and seated us with him in the
heavenly places in Christ Jesus. (Ephesians
2:5–6)

Praise God for our eternal security as His precious sheep. We
have been saved from the foundation of the world—before we were
even born. In the present there is acceptance, newness of life and no
condemnation (Romans 8:1). From God's viewpoint, our future in
heaven is a present reality. Ferguson captures the significance of the
foresight in God's plan for our salvation.

> To understand how the Bible as a whole
> works, we need to understand this riddle: The
> invisible is more substantial than the visible. The
> future comes before the past. The new is more
> fundamental than the old. What does all this
> mean? Simply put, it means that the story of the
> Lord Jesus, His person and work, is not a divine
> afterthought, a heavenly "plan b" hurriedly
> scrambled together when "plan a" went horribly
> wrong in Eden. No, the coming of Christ was in
> the plan before the Fall. Everything that precedes
> it chronologically actually follows it logically.[55]

Each of these three pictures beautifully illustrate how God alone
accomplishes our salvation and eternally secures it. As you meditate
on these; "promises in pictures," there may be one that particularly
resonates. That personal connection to a particular picture of salvation, even if you cannot fully understand or articulate why, will serve
as the link to the next topic.

---

[55] Sinclair Ferguson, "Salvation, Past, Present and Future" (Orlando; Ligonier
Ministries), February 2004, Tabletalk.

Possessing the promises

It was mentioned prior that the obstacles of *unbiblical in foundation* and *undisciplined in mind* needed to be addressed together since scriptural truth regarding salvation must be comprehended as well as apprehended in the mind. Regarding the apprehension, or claiming of the promise of salvation, there are unconscious beliefs that can hinder one's ability to lay hold of these promises personally. Psychologists refer to such counterproductive ideas, as "negative core beliefs."

Core beliefs are deeply held beliefs people have about themselves, the world, and others. Such beliefs are formed early on in life, and greatly influenced by our upbringing and experiences. Because they are embedded from early in life, they are difficult to change. In fact, most people rarely articulate them, and are often unaware of their existence. Peter Burrow, who has done extensive research on core beliefs, particularly with their application in the business world, offers physiologic reason core beliefs can be so difficult to alter.

> The cognitive process is centered in the neo-cortex (which allows us to think about thinking), while core beliefs arise from the amygdala (which acts like an internal watchdog scanning the environment for threats). Thus, because core beliefs are based on a chemical or instinctual reaction they can only be changed slowly and over a great deal of time.[56]

Furthermore, Burrow points out that despite not being closely related to facts, core beliefs are strongly (but irrationally) held, and the cognitive mind is normally used to justify rather than question them. Though their original purpose is to help us make sense of our experiences, core beliefs often become counterproductive as we become adults, and in the case of the subject at hand, they may

---

[56] Peter Burrow, *Core Beliefs* (Milton, QLD; Burrow and Associates, 2012), 8.

hinder us from experiencing assurance. Therefore, the negative core beliefs we carry with us from childhood through our adult lives must be addressed accordingly. Paul speaks to this need in his letter to the Corinthians.

> When I was a child, I spoke like a child, I thought like a child, I reasoned like a child. When I became a man, I gave up childish ways. (1 Corinthians 13:11)

> Brothers, do not be children in your thinking. Be infants in evil, but in your thinking be mature. (1 Corinthians 14:20)

Dr. Judith Beck proposed three main categories of negative core beliefs that people have about themselves.[57] Each belief is centered on the idea of either helplessness, unlovability or worthlessness. Core beliefs associated with "helplessness" are linked closely with feelings of incompetence, inferiority, and defenselessness. The core belief of "unlovability" includes false ideas and fears that we are not likeable, or incapable and unworthy of meaningful relationships. Finally, "worthlessness" core beliefs manifest in feelings of insignificance and even innate and unalterable immorality. Below is a chart of those beliefs with common themes related to each.

Helpless Core Beliefs	Unlovable Core Beliefs	Worthless Core Beliefs
I am powerless.	I am unlovable.	I am worthless.
I am a victim.	I am unwanted.	I am a waste.
I am trapped.	I am odd.	I am toxic.
I am out of control.	I am ugly.	I am evil.
I will fail.	I will be rejected.	I don't deserve to live.

---

57 Judith Beck, *Cognitive Behavioral Therapy, Basics and Beyond* 3rd ed. (New York; The Guilford Press 2021), 33.

Take a few moments to carefully read the dominant themes under each of the three negative core beliefs. Just as with the pictures of salvation, chances are that one of these negative core beliefs resonates more than the others. Though you may not understand why at this point, your negative core beliefs may have drawn you to a specific picture of salvation.

For example, a person who identifies with the negative core belief of "helplessness" may also connect more with the "secured lamb" imagery of salvation. For such individuals, seeing themselves as sheep that are taken care of by Jesus, the Great Shepherd of our souls, is most comforting. This picture speaks to specific themes of their core belief of being weak or a victim. The chronological aspects of salvation that I provided alongside this picture are also very helpful. Understanding one is eternally secure—past, present, and future— touches upon the fear of being out of control, which is a central concern for those with this core belief pattern.

Similarly, the negative core belief of "unlovability" may be paired with the, "beloved son" picture of salvation that Paul often used. People struggling with this negative core belief about themselves are drawn to the beauty of this imagery. They long to see that they are not unwanted or unlovable. They have a Father in heaven who would not spare His own Son to adopt them. They are not odd or different, but heirs of Abraham and sons and daughters of God.

Finally, the picture of salvation put forth by John of believers being a "priceless gift," may find more relevance for believers whose primary negative core belief revolves around issues of worthlessness. As mentioned, deep down, these people struggle to recognize any inherent value or goodness in themselves. Visualizing themselves as a precious gift presented to Christ by the Father is medicine for souls that struggle with feelings of worthlessness and toxicity. The great care and protection provided by each member of the Godhead to see that the gift (themselves) is endowed with eternal life and safely delivered home to heaven puts the lie to any notion that they do not deserve to live life to the fullest and be happy.

Regarding these pictures of salvation, it is very interesting that Jesus referred to each in the three parables He told the Pharisees to describe God's great love for sinners (Luke 15). Christ begins with the parable of the lost sheep, an unmistakable allusion to the *secured lamb* picture of salvation. Jesus then affirms the *precious gift* motif with the parable of the lost coin. Finally, the LORD concludes with the parable of the prodigal son, or the *beloved son* picture, which Mark Twain described as the greatest short story ever told! Take a few moments and read those parables now before continuing with our game plan.

Beck would acknowledge that it is possible for people to have elements of all three categories of negative core beliefs present within them, as well as one or multiple dominant themes within a certain category.[58] Therefore, meditation on each of the three pictures of salvation is beneficial to challenge negative core beliefs with the Word of God and enhance our ability to apprehend the promises of salvation.

It has been mentioned several times that people struggling with assurance can often have periods of confidence regarding their salvation. However, at certain critical periods of change or crisis in their lives the old fears return. If the circumstances of those stressors are significant, their specific negative core beliefs will be triggered and may cause issues with assurance-doubt to reemerge. Beck explains:

> For most of their lives, most people may maintain relatively positive core beliefs (e.g., "I am substantially in control"; "I can do most things competently"; "I am a functional human being"; "I am likable"; "I am worthwhile"). Negative core beliefs may surface only during times of psychological distress.[59]

I have been periodically including the unique challenges people with OCD must overcome to attain assurance, and it's appropriate to do so again. As Beck mentioned, the activation of core beliefs during

---

[58] Ibid., p. 286.
[59] Ibid., 166.

times of stress is a challenge we all must deal with, but people with OCD often find such periods more difficult and prolonged.

As noted earlier, there are three areas of the brain that are implicated in OCD; the orbitofrontal cortex, anterior cingulate cortex (gyrus), and the caudate nucleus. Dr. Daniel Amen explains physiologically why dysfunction of the anterior cingulate gyrus in individuals with OCD can be especially problematic during times of stress, that is, when negative core beliefs are operative.

> When the ACG was overactive and when there may be low availability of serotonin in people struggling to shift their attention, they ended up stuck on certain thoughts or behaviors... Being able to cope with change, go with the flow, and successfully handle life's little (or big) emergencies is a function of the ACG.[60]

From our discussion on fear, you'll recall that in response to overwhelming circumstances (where negative core beliefs are activated), the brain may distract itself from facing such crises. The brain does this by creating false realities more frightening than the difficult true realities it is presented with. This explains why the old reliable fears: "What if God has abandoned me?"; "What if I'm not saved?"; "What if I commit the unpardonable sin?"; "What if I go crazy?"; "What if I hurt somebody?" may surface during times of great stress. The possible "what-ifs" are endless, but each can have a devastating effect on assurance. As mentioned, such distracting intrusive thoughts are quite common in individuals with OCD.

Whether you have OCD or not, it is critical to understand the negative core beliefs that are most relevant to you. To that end, your mid-chapter Mindful question assignment will be to complete the negative core beliefs inventory assessment. Take your time and answer the questions honestly. Remember that negative core beliefs

---

[60] Daniel Amen, *Change Your Brain, Change Your Life* (New York; Harmony Books, 2015), 207, 73.

only become active under psychological distress. If that does not describe your present condition, try to imagine a time in your life that was very stressful. Do your best to recall how you perceived that situation, the emotions you felt, and your behavior during that time before you complete the assessment. Such inventories have been proven to be reliable and valid to assess negative core beliefs and validate Beck's cognitive model.[61] For continued study on negative core beliefs, I highly recommend the cited work from Dr. Judith Beck.

Negative core beliefs inventory

Please read the following statements carefully and indicate how well they describe you by choosing *one* of the four response options below. Indicate your answers in the appropriate space to the right of each statement.

1-------------------2-------------------3-------------------4
Does not describe me well   **Describes me very well**

PART 1: HOW I SEE MYSELF

1. I feel like other people are more competent than I am.	
2. I feel incompetent in most things I do.	
3. I feel inferior to some people.	
4. I think I don't measure up to others.	
5. I feel unprotected regarding life's difficulties.	

---

[61] Flávio Osmo, MSc; Victor Duran; Amy Wenzel, PhD; Irismar Reis de Oliveira, MD, PhD; Sara Nepomuceno; Maryana Madeira; Igor Menezes, PhD, "The Negative Core Beliefs Inventory: Development and Psychometric Properties," *Journal of Cognitive Psychotherapy* 32, Issue 1 (April 2018): DOI: 10.1891/0889-8391.32.1.67

6. I feel helpless when I find myself alone.	
7. I feel a sense of insecurity most of the time.	
8. I feel weak when I face adversity or a setback.	
9. I need someone I trust nearby when facing new situations.	
10. I think it's difficult for someone to like me.	
11. I feel I'm boring or uninteresting.	
12. I feel like I will always be rejected when my flaws are perceived.	
13. I feel that I will hardly ever have the love or friendship I would like from others.	
14. I think I'm not good enough to be loved.	
15. I think nobody loves me.	
16. I feel incapable of changing my life.	
17. Taking everything into account, I think I'm a failure.	
18. I feel I have little value as a person.	
19. I think my presence is harmful to others.	
20. I feel insignificant.	
21. I think the world would be better if I didn't exist.	

PART 2: HOW I SEE OTHERS

1.	I think people try to avoid me when I ask for something.
2.	I think people don't worry about saying something that might hurt me.
3.	I am afraid to open up to people and that they'll end up playing with my feelings.
4.	I feel that people hurt me on purpose.
5.	I feel I need to protect myself from others.
6.	I think people don't worry about hurting me in order to get what they need.
7.	I'm afraid to be betrayed even by someone I trust.
8.	When someone criticizes me, I feel that he/she is trying to attack me.
9.	I think people want me to fail.
10.	In many situations, I feel that people want to take advantage of me.
11.	I feel that people try to impose their ideas or opinions on me.

Instructions for calculation and interpretation of scores:

Dimensions and Subdimensions	Items	Level of Beliefs		
		Low	Medium	High
Negative core beliefs about others	1 to 11 (How I see others)	Up to 1.82	Above 1.82 to 2.45	Above 2.45
Negative core beliefs about the self	1 to 21 (How I see myself)	Up to 1.62	Above 1.62 to 2.29	Above 2.29
Helplessness/ inferiority	1 to 4 (How I see myself)	Up to 2.00	Above 2.00 to 2.75	Above 2.75
Helplessness/ vulnerability	5 to 9 (How I see myself)	Up to 2.00	Above 2.00 to 2.80	Above 2.80
Unlovability	10 to 15 (How I see myself)	Up to 1.33	Above1.33 to 2.17	Above 2.17
Worthlessness	16 to 21 (How I see myself)	Up to 1.17	Above 1.17 to 1.67	Above 1.67

Note: Scores are calculated from the average of the responses of the items.

The above inventory is a very effective tool to quickly uncover your negative core beliefs. However, refuting and changing your negative core beliefs takes time and focused effort, so you will need to soldier through the "enchanted ground." The process may also involve some emotional and psychological distress, requiring you to boldly face the "lion's den." Therefore, make sure you have your spiritual armor on. Though the process of uncovering and challenging negative core beliefs with biblical truth can be difficult, it is perhaps the most critical step in tearing down the spiritual stronghold of assurance-doubt. As Jesus said, "You will know the truth, and the truth will set you free," (John 8:32b).

2.   *Evidences of salvation and errors in thinking*

Evidences of salvation

It was mentioned earlier that God supplies two separate provisions to aid our assurance. The descriptive explanations of the promises of eternal security have been addressed along with the psychological reasons certain individuals may struggle to possess or claim those promises for themselves.

Next the evidences of salvation identified in the Bible will be discussed. However, as with the preceding topic of negative core beliefs, undisciplined thinking patterns, that psychologists refer to as cognitive distortions, can also prevent us from experiencing the assurance of salvation. Thus, after listing the biblical evidences of salvation, attention will turn to these distorted thinking patterns that can cause believers to misread or even dismiss the proofs of the salvation they possess.

Several years ago, Sinclair Ferguson participated in a live question and answer event sponsored by Ligonier Ministries. The question posed to Dr. Ferguson was, "How do I know I am saved?" In other words, what evidence should be examined to determine if genuine salvation is present? Below is Ferguson's answer.

> You know that you are saved because salvation begins to appear in your life. You desire new and different things. The Law of God that you regarded as an enemy and an irritation becomes a friend, and you want to keep it. You want to please Christ rather than let Him down. All of these are very simple things. You begin to love the people who love the Lord Jesus.
>
> These are the kind of things that 1 John speaks about. A good exercise would be to read 1 John, which speaks about our relationship to Christ, our new relationship to sin (we no longer love it, but instead hate it), and our new rela-

tionship to God's people. We begin to love God's
people and want to be with them.[62]

According to Ferguson, the evidences of salvation are both
internal and external. Not only will our desires change as a result of
saving faith, but those desires will also manifest in obedient deeds of
righteousness. The impact of the periodic deficiency of these external
and internal evidences have on assurance was addressed in discussion
of the first two obstacles, *uncommitted in walk* and *unrestored in emotions*,
so no further comments in that regard are necessary. However,
MacArthur fills in the details of those internal and external changes
Ferguson alluded to by identifying nine separate conditions from the
Bible that prove genuine saving faith.[63]

Time will not be spent to develop each evidence other than
to call attention to God's central role in producing and recognizing
these evidences. It is the presence of the Holy Spirit within us that
brings these seeds of salvation into full bloom. He uses the Word of
God as a tool to not only to mature us in the faith but also to help us
recognize our growth as an encouragement for us.

To that end, I have included relevant prooftexts from Scripture
that support the list provided by MacArthur as well as cited the article
for you to access for further study. Below are the biblical marks
of true conversion identified by MacArthur with supporting passages
that I have added.

1. Love for God. (Matthew 10:37–39)
2. Repentance from sin. (Proverbs 28:13; Matthew 3:8)
3. Genuine humility. (Matthew 18:3)
4. Devotion to God's glory (1 Corinthians 10:31; 2 Peter 1:6)
5. Continual prayer. (Psalm 32:6; 69:13; Job 22:27; Romans 12:12; Philippians 4:5–7)
6. Selfless love. (1 John 3:14,17; 2 Peter 1:7)

---

[62] Sinclair Ferguson, "How do I Know if I am Saved?" (Orlando; Ligonier Ministries).

[63] John MacArthur, What kind of things do and do not prove the genuineness of saving faith? © 2023 Grace to You. All rights reserved. Grace to You, gty.org.

7. Separation from the world. (Ephesians 2:1–3; Colossians 1:13; James 4:4)
8. Spiritual growth. (Philippians 1:6; 2 Peter 1:8)
9. Obedience. (Ephesians 2:10; 1 Peter 1:2)

Errors in thinking

If one has errors in his thinking, he can look at such a list and come away more discouraged than ever. His doubts concerning his own salvation are only magnified after seeing such a list in an "all-or-none" manner. MacArthur recognized this possibility for despair.

> Without question Christians fail in each of these areas, but the direction of a Christian's life is to love God, hate sin, to live in humility and self-denial, recognizing his unworthiness and being devoted to the glory of God. It is not the perfection of one's life but the direction of a life that provides evidence of regeneration.[64]

Christians who never or rarely struggle with assurance, can look at the list provided by MacArthur and immediately deduce that perfection in any evidence is an impossibility. However, for individuals who do struggle, their minds may latch on to one or more of those evidences.

They may over-analyze and hyper-focus on a specific proof, especially one that elicits an emotional response in them. They often compare themselves to other Christians they admire, which inevitably increases their doubt. They also set unrealistic expectations upon themselves, and assume God does the same.

As mentioned, these are all thinking errors that psychologists call cognitive distortions. Cognitive distortions are negative thinking patterns that aren't based on fact or reality. They are formed ulti-

---

[64] Ibid., "Proof of Salvation."

mately from the negative core beliefs we hold, which is another reason I am so insistent that you identify your negative core beliefs.

Dr. Schwartz identifies eight cognitive distortions that affect everyone from time to time and to varying degrees.[65] Below is a chart that Dr. Schwartz uses with patients to identify thinking errors present in their life.

I will fill in the chart as a person struggling with assurance may interpret MacArthur's evidences of salvation list. Under each cognitive distortion I also include a Bible verse that when memorized and meditated upon will help replace such thinking errors with the truth of Scripture.

Thinking Error	Example(s) and Where They Occur (or with Whom)	Result
1. All or nothing *Not that I have already obtained this or am already perfect, but I press on to make it my own, because Christ Jesus has made me his own... Let those of us who are mature think this way, and if in anything you think otherwise, God will reveal that also to you.* (Philippians 3:12;15)	I still struggle from time to time with lust; I must not be saved.	Worthless and evil... I am never satisfied with my progress as a Christian.

---

[65] Ibid., *You are not Your Brain*, 200–220.

2. Catastrophizing *"For I know the plans I have for you," declares the LORD, "plans to prosper you and not to harm you, plans to give you hope and a future."* (Jeremiah 29:11)	I had blasphemous thoughts in church this morning. God is going to send me to hell for allowing such thoughts to pop into my head.	Exhausted… I am worn out from constantly worrying about my salvation.
3. Discounting the positive *Finally, brothers and sisters, whatever is true, whatever is noble, whatever is right, whatever is pure, whatever is lovely, whatever is admirable—if anything is excellent or praiseworthy—think about such things.* (Philippians 4:8)	I misunderstood that passage of Scripture the pastor covered this morning. If I was truly saved the Holy Spirit would have revealed that to me.	Not good enough… Why didn't the Holy Spirit reveal this to me?
4. Emotional reasoning *Trust in the LORD with all your heart, and do not lean on your own understanding. In all your ways acknowledge him, and he will make straight your paths.* (Proverbs 3:5–6)	I feel out of control, what if I commit the unpardonable sin?	Trapped… No matter how much I pray, I can't seem to stop worrying that I may one day lose my salvation.

5. Mind reading *For my thoughts are not your thoughts, neither are your ways my ways, declares the LORD.* *For as the heavens are higher than the earth, so are my ways higher than your ways and my thoughts than your thoughts.* (Isaiah 55:8)	I have not struggled with assurance for a while, but since I started this new job, those old fears have returned. God is punishing me for not trusting Him.	Frustrated… I must try to figure out what I'm doing wrong and why God is angry with me.
6. "Should" statements *But with me it is a very small thing that I should be judged by you or by any human court. In fact, I do not even judge myself.* (1 Corinthians 4:3)	I'm too worldly. I shouldn't be listening to this music; maybe that's why I have no assurance?	Disappointed… I should be more mature by now, I should spend more time in prayer.
7. Faulty comparisons *We do not dare to classify or compare ourselves with some who commend themselves. When they measure themselves by themselves and compare themselves with themselves, they are not wise.* (2 Corinthians 10:12)	I have been a Christian longer than her, yet she does more for the church.	Inadequate… I am not pushing myself hard enough. If I do, then maybe my assurance will return.

8. False expectations	If God truly loves me, He will take away my arrogant attitude I have towards certain people at work.	Abandoned… A true Christian should never have these types of attitudes. This is why I have no assurance.
No temptation has overtaken you except what is common to mankind. And God is faithful; he will not let you be tempted beyond what you can bear. But when you are tempted, he will also provide a way out so that you can endure it. (1 Corinthians 10:13)		

Though these responses are hypothetical, they are not unrealistic. Many people who struggle with assurance may record answers very similar to these. Perhaps you picked up on the influence one's negative core beliefs has on these faulty thinking patterns? The themes of helplessness, unlovability and worthlessness give rise to these cognitive distortions and manifest themselves in the hypothetical responses I listed.

Review

Remember that negative core beliefs can be triggered during times of great stress in a person's life. Moreover, the cognitive distortions that arise from those negative core beliefs determine how we interpret and respond to the challenging circumstances. If we struggle with assurance-doubt, such periods of stress can worsen our condition.

The import of Paul's charge to the Corinthians to take every thought captive is made abundantly clear when we visually see the progression from:

major life stressor → negative core beliefs →
cognitive distortions → negative emotional and

behavioral effects → formation/strengthening of
the spiritual stronghold of assurance-doubt.

Understanding how spiritual strongholds are formed and
strengthened is so very critical, that it warrants sharing these verses
one more time.

> For the weapons of our warfare are not of
> the flesh but have divine power to destroy strong-
> holds. We destroy arguments and every lofty
> opinion raised against the knowledge of God,
> and take every thought captive to obey Christ. (2
> Corinthians 10:4–5)

Negative core beliefs and distorted thinking patterns (cognitive distortions), as well as incomplete or flawed knowledge of the
Scriptures are the thoughts that need to be taken captive for assurance to be apprehended as well as comprehended. Again, this is the
reason I chose to discuss the obstacles of *unbiblical in foundation* and
undisciplined in mind simultaneously. Thus, for assurance to be realized, both obstacles must be overcome. For example, let's first look
at the example of believers who only fail to overcome the obstacle of
undisciplined in mind.

Negative core beliefs and cognitive distortions are symptoms of
an undisciplined mind. Both have detrimental effects on one's ability to personally apprehend the promises and evidences of salvation
necessary to attain assurance. As Groeschel rightly observes, "Lies
believed about ourselves to be true, will affect our lives as if they were
true."[66]

Such individuals may understand all the correct doctrines of
eternal security, be an obedient believer with no significant unresolved emotional issues yet still lack assurance. They may even go
long periods of time with relatively little doubt regarding their sal-

---

[66] Craig Groeschel, *Winning the War in Your Mind* (Grand Rapids; Zondervan
Books, 2021), 13.

vation. For these individuals, it is only during periods of great stress, do struggles with assurance resurface. Stress triggers their negative core beliefs and cognitive distortions, which then impacts their emotions and actions. The TEA graph below is a representation of such believers.

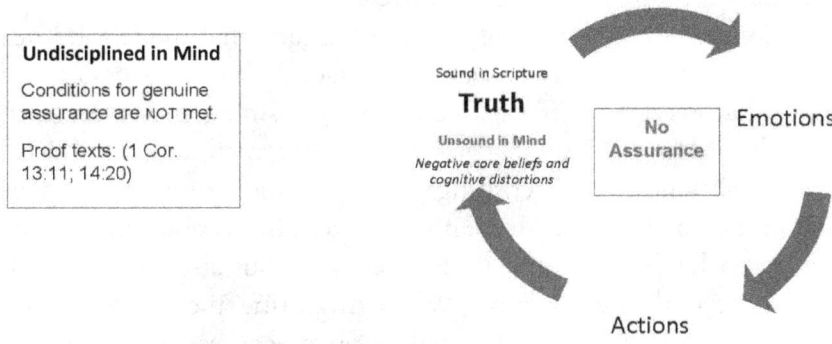

A misunderstanding of all the facets of salvation explained in the Bible also impacts one's assurance, even in the absence of distorted thinking patterns, gross negligence, or major unresolved emotional issues.

Because of their misunderstanding of Scripture, such individuals fail to overcome the obstacle of *unbiblical in foundation* and will inevitably have periodic struggles with assurance. Moreover, it is impossible for them to ever have a lasting assurance, as long as they remain ignorant of, or deny of the doctrine of eternal security. I will explain next why that is impossible, but to do so requires a brief history lesson.

To begin, you may have heard of people who deny eternal security referred to as "Arminians." This is because the Dutch theologian; Jacobus Arminius championed this belief in his debates with John Calvin. However, this disagreement over eternal security; did not originate with them, but with Augustine and Pelagius centuries before. I will not take the time to fully develop the history of their debate other than briefly explain how each man's view of the consequences of the fall directly influenced his understanding of eternal security.

In short, Augustine, and Calvin after him, firmly taught that because of the total depravity of man after the fall we are not only incapable of coming to faith in our own strength but are equally impotent to persevere in our own strength. Therefore, God must grant us salvation and eternally secure it.

Conversely, Pelagius and Arminius argued that the fall did not result in the total depravity of man. In fact, Pelagius went so far as to say that every man is capable of living a sinless life in his own strength and he held to the belief that some men actually did so. God's preserving grace, according to Pelagius and Arminius is dependent on man's obedience. If man is negligent in his obedience to the faith, then he forfeits not only his assurance but also his salvation. This is the critical distinction! While Augustine and Calvin would agree that assurance is in part based on obedience, security is not. As the Puritan preacher, William Jenkins wisely observed, "sin can never quite bereave a saint of his jewel, his grace; but it may steal away the key of the cabinet, his assurance!

Arminian views on eternal security may be found in most Methodist, Free Will Baptist, and Pentecostal denominations. Whereas, Reformed Protestant denominations would hold to eternal security as championed by Calvin, and Augustine before him. Presbyterian, and most Baptist and Independent churches, would fall in this camp.

These examples of churches and denominations who espouse or deny eternal security is not exhaustive or infallible. Therefore, I would advise you to determine where your church and pastor fall with respect to the doctrine of eternal salvation. Whether you agree or disagree with Geisler's differentiation between strong and moderate Calvinism, his summary of the different views on eternal security between Calvinists and Arminians is spot-on.[67]

---

[67] Ibid., 67.

VIEWS ON ETERNAL SECURITY	
Moderate Calvinism	**Arminianism**
All believers have it.	No believers have it.
No believer can lose it.	Any believer can lose it.
It cannot be lost by our actions.	It can be lost by our actions.
God gives assurance and security.	God gives assurance but no security.

As important as the doctrine of eternal security is, I would stop short of saying that adherence to it is prerequisite for genuine salvation. In fact, there are many Christians who do not believe in eternal security. Nevertheless, I do believe that the Arminian view of eternal security cannot be supported by the whole of Scripture, the character of God, the fallenness of man, and the absolute necessity of grace. Moreover, the four aspects of our salvation: election, justification, sanctification, and glorification would all have to be radically redefined if the doctrine of eternal security was not true. Therefore, I would caution against attending a church that denies eternal security at least until you are well grounded in your assurance.

It would have been clearer if Geisler explained that those who deny eternal security can experience no *"lasting"* assurance, because at any time in the future due to some undefined disobedience they may lose their salvation. Below is graphic representation of believers, who can expect no lasting assurance because they have yet to overcome the obstacle of *unbiblical in foundation.*

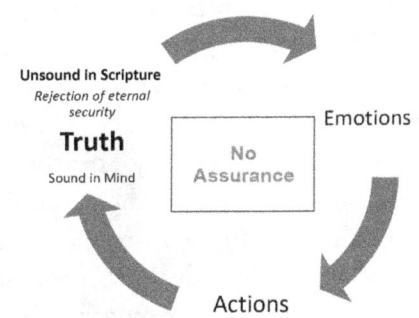

Unbiblical in Foundation

Conditions for genuine assurance are NOT met.

Proof texts: (Numerous: See discussion on Precious Promises)

Unsound in Scripture
Rejection of eternal security
Truth
Sound in Mind

No
Assurance

Emotions

Actions

Final thoughts: Putting it all together

Discussion of the four obstacles specific to the spiritual strong-hold of assurance-doubt—*uncommitted in walk, unrestored in emotions, unbiblical in foundation*, and *undisciplined in mind*—is now complete. I said early on that this book was not an autobiography, and I certainly don't want to turn it into one now at the stroke of midnight in our game plan!

However, I also said that I successfully walked through each of these obstacles to assurance, and wanted to help you do the same. Therefore, I believe my experience will help you understand how these obstacles to assurance can manifest in a believer's life and be subsequently overcome.

Briefly then, a few years after I came to faith as a young man, I fell into a backslidden state that lasted for about two years. My assurance suffered greatly as a result of this period of disobedience, but once I returned to the Lord, my assurance was restored. I realized from the study of 2 Peter and other books of the Bible the great impact obedience has on assurance. Thus, *uncommitted in walk* was the first obstacle I had to overcome in my battles with assurance-doubt.

However, during that backslidden season, I committed grievous sins and made some very foolish decisions that greatly wounded my conscience. Some of those sinful actions produced lasting consequences, that had more of an impact on me emotionally than I was aware of at the time. It took some very stressful situations in my life, to finally surface the full weight of those emotions.

Amid this period of stress, my assurance mysteriously started to suffer again, even though I was not negligent or disobedient in my walk. I began to get very anxious, the old fears of committing the unpardonable sin returned and as a result I was in a most miserable state.

However, the Holy Spirit was using this trial to force me back into the lion's den, to thoroughly deal with the negative emotions that still clung to me from that regretful time of my life. Like David, once I dealt biblically with the guilt and shame of my past, the joy of my salvation was restored. Therefore, *unrestored in emotions*, was the second obstacle to assurance I overcame, and at the time I was convinced it would be the last. I was mistaken.

Several years later a still greater challenge occurred in my life that brought on a new wave of assurance-doubts. The old intrusive blasphemous thoughts that I was sure would never return were back in full force. I also endured what I believed was a severe form of what the divines referred to as sudden vehement temptations—a truly horrific experience that I will not elaborate on. This was the most difficult wave of assurance-doubt I have ever experienced. The reemergence of these excruciating conditions and doubts confused me, and quite frankly angered me!

I was living an obedient life and had no need of further emotional closure. In fact, by this time I was a deacon in the church and seminary student. I was even counseling others with regards to their assurance struggles. The more I thought about what I deemed the unfairness of my condition, the angrier I got with God for allowing this to happen to me again.

However, at this stage of my life, I was unaware of the reality of negative core beliefs, let alone the ones that influenced me, nor was I aware of the cognitive distortions that characterized my thinking most. Unbeknownst to me, it was the activation of my negative core beliefs brought on by this extreme stress in my life that was responsible for this intense reawakening of the spiritual stronghold of assurance-doubt. Below is a graphic representation of how this process unfolded in my life.

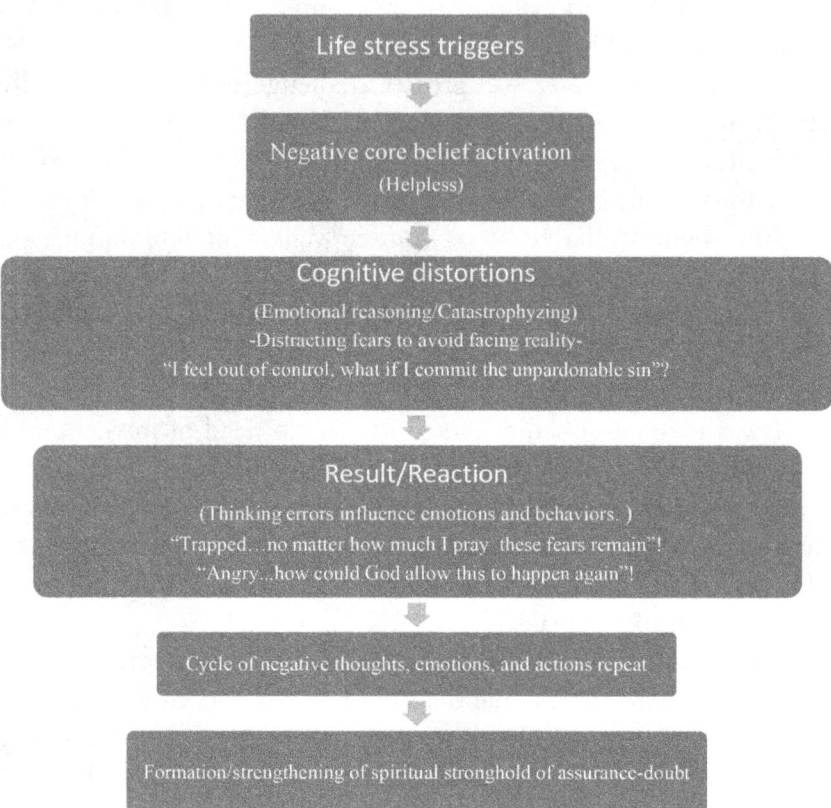

Despite my misplaced anger and resentment, God put some wise counselors in my life who made me aware of how my negative core beliefs and cognitive distortions influenced my response to stressful situations. They also helped me to understand why my struggles with assurance worsened during these tumultuous periods.

It was revelatory when I realized that these distracting fears and doubts concerning my salvation emerged from the triggering of negative core beliefs and cognitive distortions from the stresses of life. From that point on, I was determined to learn all I could on the subject from a scriptural and scientific perspective. I also sought to uncover my own negative core beliefs and cognitive distortions. I began to understand how they developed and the impact they had throughout the course of my life.

Though I always believed, or perhaps a better word is hoped that the doctrine of eternal security was true I nonetheless had periodic doubts. Therefore, I also began an intensive study on the doctrine salvation and the various views on eternal security. This focused study on negative core beliefs, cognitive distortions and eternal security eventually led me to the realization that the eternal promises of salvation must be both comprehended and apprehended if assurance is to be maintained. This is especially true during periods of high stress! Thus, I came to see that there were two more obstacles to assurance that must be overcome: *unbiblical in foundation* and *undisciplined in mind.*

As I examined the three categories of negative core beliefs (helpless, worthless, and unlovable) I saw how the destructive themes of each were addressed by the three pictures of salvation I observed that were put forth in Scripture (secured lamb, precious gift and beloved son). I also realized how the cognitive distortions which arise from negative core beliefs hamper our ability to correctly assess and acknowledge the evidences of salvation present within our own lives.

Armed with this knowledge, as new stresses occurred, I refuted the negative core beliefs and cognitive distortions those challenges triggered by meditating on the "promises in pictures" that resonated with my specific negative core beliefs. I also disciplined my mind by taking captive the cognitive distortions that characterized my thinking most, stayed focused on the real problem, and brought it to God in prayer. When I followed this strategy, my mind no longer needed to distract itself with fearful blasphemous thoughts. Though such intrusive thoughts still occasionally occurred their frequency and intensity were less severe. In fact, the presence of such thoughts lingered simply as a memory of my experience with them or undealt with low levels of stress and negative emotions. Regarding the latter two, I now see intrusive thoughts as a very effective alarm that something very important to me is amiss in my life or my walk with the LORD that requires me to take appropriate action. Dr. Lauren

Edwards, psychiatrist for the University of Nebraska Medical Center, confirms that intrusive thoughts play a significant role in this regard.

> "Intrusive thoughts tend to reflect our greatest fears or most unwanted scenarios, so you can treat it as a signal of something important to you," Dr. Edwards says. "If a new mother is having the intrusive thought of drowning her baby in the bath, which is not uncommon, it's a manifestation of her connection to this little vulnerable creature who is so fragile and dependent upon her for safety."[68]

It is very important for those with OCD to be aware of the possibility for the remaining, albeit waning presence of intrusive thoughts, or thought-action fusion. Even when you have overcome each obstacle of assurance-doubt, such symptoms of OCD may linger on in a weakened state and be exacerbated during times of great stress. Such calamitous times may negatively impact your assurance until you have dealt fully with your negative core beliefs. Indeed, the WCF affirms that "true believers may have the assurance of their salvation divers ways shaken, diminished, and intermitted."

If you are a Lord of the Rings fan, think of these waning symptoms as Frodo's wound from a Mordor blade. You will survive and be the stronger for it, but the wound may never fully heal. If you are not an LOTR fan, and that reference makes no sense to you, take heart then that even Bunyan, after he had won his assurance still occasionally dealt with such symptoms. Though they were more severe for Bunyan because he did not understand his own condition, they

---

[68] Nebraska Medicine, Behavioral Health, "What are intrusive thoughts, and are they normal?" June 13, 2023.

nonetheless decreased in their frequency. Listen to his own account from *Grace Abounding.*

> Sometimes when I have been preaching, I have been violently assaulted with thoughts of blasphemy and have been strongly tempted to speak those words to the congregation. There have been times when I have begun to speak the Word with much clearness, evidence, and liberty of speech, yet before the end of the message I was so blinded and estranged from the things I had been speaking, and have also been so limited in my speech as to utterance before the people, that it was if I had not known or remembered what I had been speaking about, or as if my head was in a bag all the time of the sermon.[69]

To finish the telling of my experience, by overcoming the obstacles of *unbiblical in foundation* and *undisciplined in mind* in this manner, I was able to face some significant life challenges and maintain my assurance, though not without struggle or assistance! Remember, don't equate success with a lack of profound struggle at times. Jesus sweated great drops of blood in His struggle in Gethsemane, and despite being God Incarnate, He humbly accepted angelic aid to His human nature. To be very clear, the angels played no part in the salvific work of Christ. They experienced none of Christ's agony, and even the strongest angelic creature could not atone for a single sin. Oh, the infinite love, strength, determination, and humility of the omnipotent Son of God! Therefore, in your personal struggle with assurance-doubt, don't be too proud to ask for and accept help, "for God opposes the proud but gives grace to the humble" (1 Peter 5:5b).

---

[69] Ibid., 122.

Below is a visual depiction of my management of subsequent life stressors.

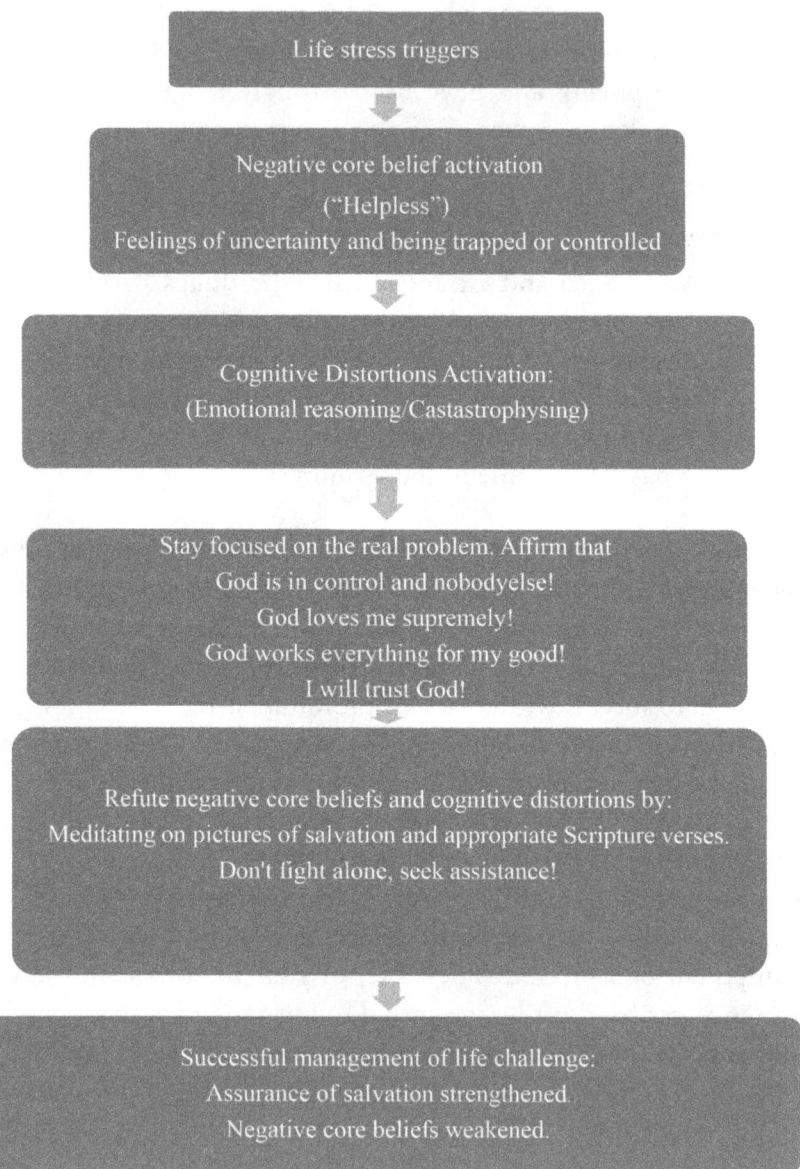

I hope the sharing of my experience has helped you understand how each of these obstacles are synergistically connected. More importantly, I hope you are encouraged and confident to replicate the same strategies in your own struggle for assurance. Don't get discouraged or disillusioned when (not if) you falter following this strategy during a significant life crisis. I have struggled profoundly at times, but each time, I learned new lessons about the majesty of Christ and my own uncertainties.

Remember, the best football coaches and game plans don't produce blowout victories every game. Sometimes in football, we face opponents that are more than we can handle. When that happens in your trials of life, dust yourself off and get back in the fight. Our struggles with feelings of helplessness, worthlessness, and unlovability will improve if we are humble enough to acknowledge them and determined enough to combat them with the truth of God. We will never be perfect in this life, but we will make considerable progress. So stay committed to the game plan and don't ever quit! Even the great apostle Paul near the end of his life acknowledged that he was still a work in progress.

> Not that I have already obtained this or am already perfect, but I press on to make it my own because Christ Jesus has made me His own.
>
> Brothers, I do not consider that I have made it my own. But one thing I do: Forgetting what lies behind and straining forward to what lies ahead, I press on toward the goal for the prize of the upward call of God in Christ Jesus.
>
> Let those of us who are mature think this way, and if in anything you think otherwise, God will reveal that also to you. (Philippians 3:13–15)

I have some final considerations specifically for my OCD brothers and sisters. First, prayerfully reflect on the example of Elijah (1 Kings 19:1–8) and avail yourself of medicine and/or therapy if you and your physician believe it is necessary. Though God is not going to send you an angel, feed you a heavenly meal, and put you to sleep as He did for Elijah, He has providentially equipped skilled physicians and wise counselors and ordained the discovery of effective medicines. So don't be afraid to follow the advice of your medical professionals.

Secondly, remember that negative core beliefs are very difficult to change. If your negative core beliefs are born out of significant childhood dysfunction and/or trauma, you may experience struggles at times with assurance-doubt. It doesn't mean you're weak or crazy; it is simply the uniqueness of your brain being exacerbated by a particular stressor that exposes your negative core beliefs. This is why you can handle certain stresses that are extremely difficult but get shaken by others that are miniscule in comparison. So take heart that people with OCD are extremely strong and determined individuals!

Finally, always know that those fearful intrusive thoughts are egodystonic and not based on reality. If you find yourself in the throes of such an agonizing experience, God will grant you glimpses of your true self and His presence just like He did for Job during his great trial. "Thy visitation hath preserved my spirit" (Job 10:12b). When your mind clears, God will show you your true underlying fears if you ask Him and supply the grace to help you overcome them.

In conclusion, we have covered a great deal of information in our game plan for assurance that requires a final review. However, that recap will have to wait as we have one more obstacle to address. As mentioned in chapter 6, this final obstacle, *unsaved in reality*, will introduce an entirely new spiritual stronghold, that quite frankly is much more prevalent and powerful than the spiritual stronghold of assurance-doubt.

Mindful question

1. Think of the times in your life when you experienced the most psychological and emotional distress. How did your negative core beliefs influence how you responded to those events?
2. Continue to meditate on how your negative core beliefs were formed and seek counsel on how to challenge them.

10

GAME PLAN—PHASE 4:
IMPLEMENTATION

Unsaved in Reality

Since no man is excluded from calling upon God, the
gate of salvation is open to all. There is nothing else to
hinder us from entering, but our own unbelief.
—John Calvin

A different stronghold

Until now, I have been dealing exclusively with the spiritual
stronghold of assurance-doubt and the four obstacles that must be
overcome to destroy it. However, there is another spiritual stronghold identified in the Bible, often referred to as false-assurance,
whose lone obstacle to overcome is what I have designated as *unsaved
in reality*.

These two strongholds are similar in some ways but could not
be further apart in others. Unlike the stronghold of assurance-doubt
individuals held captive by the stronghold of false-assurance do not
have saving faith but think that they do. It's safe to say that more
people are held prisoner to the stronghold of false-assurance than
all others combined! Indeed, not every believer will experience the

difficulties of assurance-doubt, but every person born since the fall inherits the ramifications of false-assurance, whether they are conscious of it or not. In this regard, then, the two strongholds are polar opposites.

However, both are spiritual strongholds and as such each are strengthened by the synergy of thoughts, emotions, and actions of the "old man," exacerbated by demonic influence, and are impossible to tear down without the aid of the Holy Spirit.

In Matthew's Gospel, Jesus acknowledges the reality of people held captive by the spiritual stronghold of false-assurance and predicts their awful fate.

> Not every one that saith unto me, Lord, Lord, shall enter into the kingdom of heaven; but he that doeth the will of my Father which is in heaven.
>
> Many will say to me in that day, Lord, Lord, have we not prophesied in thy name? and in thy name have cast out devils? and in thy name done many wonderful works?
>
> And then will I profess unto them, I never knew you: depart from me, ye that work iniquity. (Matthew 7:21–23 KJV)

Again, these unfortunate souls represent Sproul's fourth category of people, those who are unsaved but think they are. Mark Twain once said, "It's easier to fool people than to convince them that they have been fooled." If that's true, then the spiritual stronghold of false-assurance will be exceedingly difficult to dismantle!

There are two main reasons people become prisoners of the stronghold of false-assurance, and both are attributed to poor theology. First there are those who believe that all people will go to heaven when they die. Regardless of the faith they had or the works they did, they believe God will grant them salvation. Theologians refer to such people as universalists. The second error is the notion that a person can earn their spot in heaven by their own good works. In fact, people who believe this would affirm that they must do good works to merit salvation. In one respect, people who think they must do work to earn salvation are correct, but they are horribly mistaken in their definition of that work.

In the above verse from Matthew, Jesus states that only those who do the will of the Father will enter into the kingdom of heaven. In other words, the will of God is the work that we must do to receive salvation. So what exactly is the will of God that we must do to make it to heaven? Jesus provides that answer in the Gospel of John.

To set the stage, Jesus had just fed the five thousand and knowing that they planned to make Him King by force following that miracle, He departed from them. However, the next day they found Jesus and asked Him where He had gone. Below is Jesus's response to the people and where He explains the work of God necessary for salvation.

> Jesus answered them and said, Verily, verily, I say unto you, Ye seek me, not because ye saw the miracles, but because ye did eat of the loaves, and were filled.
> Labour not for the meat which perisheth, but for that meat which endureth unto everlasting life, which the Son of man shall give unto you: for him hath God the Father sealed.
> Then said they unto him, What shall we do, that we might work the works of God?
> Jesus answered and said unto them, This is the work of God, that ye believe on him whom he hath sent. (John 6:26–29 KJV)

Thus, the work necessary to get to heaven is to repent from all other beliefs and believe solely in Christ, the Father who sent him, and as we shall see, the reason why he was sent. However, this begs a very important question; "What does Jesus mean by believe?" To overcome the obstacle to false-assurance, *unsaved in reality*, we must know the answer to that question.

So what does Jesus mean by *belief,* and what exactly are the specific realities associated with that belief? Is belief merely acknowledging all the orthodox teachings concerning God the Father, Son and Holy Spirit are true? Many Americans, of all religious stripes, Muslim, Jewish, and even those identifying as Christian would say that beliefs aren't enough by themselves. The prevailing thought is that salvation must also be earned or at least kept by the individual. One must receive the sacraments, keep the law, or have the scales of good works outweigh the scales of evil deeds. Others not so pious, believe that joining a church, mosque or synagogue is enough to earn a guaranteed spot in heaven. Then there are those who believe all one needs to go to Heaven, is to have "God in your heart" or to be "spiritual," whatever either of those phrases mean?

Biblical Christianity affirms that although correct understanding of biblical truth and personal holiness are critical, neither of these, alone or in unison, is sufficient to get one to heaven. To prove this statement and to subsequently explain the scriptural teaching on how one receives eternal life, I will take a page from the wisest man who ever lived, King Solomon.

In the book of Proverbs, Solomon's preferred teaching style was what Bible scholars give the fancy name, "antithetical parallelism." Antithetical parallelism is simply a style of teaching where one provides an antithesis, or contrast. Thus, verses containing antithetical parallelism will bring together opposing ideas in marked contrast to clarify its premise.

Attaining wisdom is the theme for the book of Proverbs, and Solomon states early on how wisdom is obtained, "The fear of the Lord is the beginning of knowledge, But fools despise wisdom and instruction." (Proverbs 1:7). Throughout the rest of the book, Solomon illustrates how wisdom is obtained and its benefits by contrasting wisdom in various ways with its antithesis, folly. For example, Solomon compared the righteous and the wicked, the industrious and the slothful, and the haughty and the humble, to name a few.

In Solomonic fashion, the opposing subjects I will use to discuss biblical salvation will be demons and Christians, specifically the beliefs of each, since Jesus stated that belief is the only work necessary for salvation. I will conduct this foray into "antithetical parallelism," by examining three critical beliefs necessary for salvation and see how demons and Christians compare with respect to those beliefs. Each belief comprises part of the total work of belief required by God for salvation and therefore all three beliefs are necessary.

As this discussion progresses it is important to honestly assess your own convictions regarding each belief addressed. Conducting self-scouts was an integral component in the game plan for overcoming assurance-doubt, but it is the central component in the game plan for overcoming the spiritual stronghold of false-assurance. Thus, I will provide you an opportunity to conduct your own self-scout of each belief we discuss in a separate column marked "Me?." I will begin with the basic belief in God.

I. Belief in God

> You believe that there is one God. You do well. Even the demons believe—and tremble! (James 2:19)

In the above verse, James is writing to Jewish Christians that have been scattered across the Roman empire due to persecution. As a result, some believers apparently became disenchanted from these hardships and waivered in the faith, becoming "double-minded" as James puts it (1:8;4:8). Apparently, they minimized their decline in zeal and obedience by elevating their belief in the existence of God.

We cannot assume that everyone that James was writing to were genuine believers who were simply backslidden in their walk. In fact, its highly probable that some were prisoners of the spiritual stronghold of false-assurance, as the visible church will always be a mixture of wheat and tares (Matthew 13:25–30). Therefore, it's noteworthy that both the saved and the unsaved were using the same excuse to justify their behaviors. That should not come as a surprise as we do the same thing today. We overlook our disobedience and lack of zeal by comparing our beliefs with those of the atheist, pagan, cultist, and all who don't believe in the God of the Bible.

James's response to such reasoning is very interesting. James first commends them for their belief in the existence of God, as that is the necessary starting point for faith, as the author of Hebrews affirms:

> And without faith it is impossible to please him, for whoever would draw near to God must believe that he exists and that he rewards those who seek him (Hebrews 11:6).

However, in the same breath, James retorts that even the demons believe, and shudder! Belief in the existence of God is the starting point, the foundation if you will, in the work of belief required for salvation. Regarding this foundational belief, it's interesting to understand where the majority of Americans are.

In October of 2006, the Harris Poll, a nationally known and respected poll, surveyed 2,010 adults as to their belief in God. This was a repeat of the same poll conducted in 2003. The 2006 results from this poll reveal that 73 percent of Americans believe in God but only 58 percent say they are absolutely certain in that belief. The poll was broken down generally by those identifying as either Christian or Jewish. The Christian category was further delineated by denomination, either Roman Catholic, a mainline Protestant denomination and born again (defined as, "personally accepting Jesus Christ as Savior").

Though still a majority, in just a three-year span, the percentage of Americans who claim to believe in God had declined by 6 percent. I shudder to think what these percentages are now in 2023! When looking at the category of "Absolutely Certain There is a God," the number of Americans who described their belief in that manner also dropped by 8 percent.

Sadly, based on the results of the Harris poll, a significant number of Americans are not even at "demon level" with regards to the certainty of the existence of God, let alone a God to be feared and reverenced. How tragic that 36 percent of Catholics, 24 percent of Protestants, and a whopping 70 percent of Jews cannot affirm their absolute certainty in the existence of God. What follows are the results of the Harris poll in its entirety.[70]

Beliefs Concerning God	2003 Total (%)	2006 Total (%)	Catholic (06)%	Protestant (06)%	Jewish (06)%	Born-Again Christian (06)%
Believe in God	79	73	84	90	64	97
Absolutely certain that there is a God.	66	58	64	76	30	93
Somewhat certain that there is a God.	12	15	21	14	34	4
Believe there is no God	9	11	5	3	12	3
Somewhat certain that there is no God.	5	6	3	1	8	1
Absolutely certain that there is no God.	4	6	2	2	4	2
Not sure whether there is a God	12	16	11	7	24	

As important as it is, belief in the existence of God doesn't differentiate Christians from demons, or even those who are held pris-

---

[70] The Harris Poll, Americans' Belief in God, 2006.

oners of false-assurance. Before going on to the next belief, fill out your self-scout column. It is critical that you honestly assess yourself. Are you absolutely certain that there is a God?

Beliefs	Demons	Christians	Me?
1. Belief in God.	Yes	Yes	

II. *Belief in Jesus*

> And he healed many who were sick with various diseases, and cast out many demons. And he would not permit the demons to speak, because they knew him. (Mark 1:34)

> And in the synagogue there was a man who had the spirit of an unclean demon, and he cried out with a loud voice, "Ha! What have you to do with us, Jesus of Nazareth? Have you come to destroy us? I know who you are—the Holy One of God." (Luke 4:33–34)

> And demons also came out of many, crying, "You are the Son of God!" But he rebuked them and would not allow them to speak, because they knew that he was the Christ. (Luke 4:41)

Advancing from the general belief in God, subsequent beliefs to be examined will become more specific. Belief in the deity of Jesus Christ will now be discussed. The Gospel accounts of Jesus' earthly ministry make abundantly clear that the demonic realm knew exactly who Christ was. Despite the flesh took on by Christ, the devils recognized him, and remembered him from eternity past. In fact, Peter was not the first to recognize Jesus's true identity (Luke 9:20), it was the demons!

A close reading of each of the accounts, reveal that the demons knew Jesus as, "the Holy One of God," "the Christ," and "the Son of God." These are all titles that the Jews understood as being equal in all the divine attributes of God. In fact, during Christ's sham trial before the Sanhedrin, the high priest used Christ's own self-acknowledgment of divinity to condemn him.

> But Jesus held his peace. And the high priest answered and said unto him, I adjure thee by the living God, that thou tell us whether thou be the Christ, the Son of God.
>
> Jesus saith unto him, Thou hast said: nevertheless I say unto you, Hereafter shall ye see the Son of man sitting on the right hand of power, and coming in the clouds of heaven.
>
> Then the high priest rent his clothes, saying, He hath spoken blasphemy; what further need have we of witnesses? behold, now ye have heard his blasphemy.
>
> What think ye? They answered and said, He is guilty of death. (Matthew 26:63–66 KJV)

It is interesting that the Bible records that the demons said they "knew," not "believed," who Jesus was. This is critical to understand. "Believing" and "knowing" are often used interchangeably. Yet there are important distinctions between the two that become clear when one studies the context in which they are used. Thus "knowing," the mental ascent that something is true, is not the same as belief or faith.

Faith and belief require trust and reliance. It will result in a personal change in the individual who possesses it. Though I waited to make this clarification between belief and knowledge until now, it was this very distinction that James wanted his listeners to consider when he stated, "Even the demons believe—and tremble."

Though there is a difference between knowing and believing, both are important. There are many people who claim to be Christians yet prove they do not know Christ by denying His divinity, sinlessness, resurrection, and virtually every other essential doctrine of the faith. Despite being highly regarded as a great teacher and prophet by those from other religions, they too would deny that Jesus is God, and, as a result, prove they do not know him, nor place their trust in Him.

Genuine Christians believe in (know) and on (trust) Jesus Christ, as the omnipotent Son of God and Savior of the world. Consider how Peter links the importance of correct knowledge and trusting belief in the following passage.

> Then Simon Peter answered him, Lord, to whom shall we go? Thou hast the words of eternal life. And we believe and are sure that thou art that Christ, the Son of the living God. (John 6:68–69 KJV)

Peter makes the distinction between knowing and believing. Peter uses the verb, "believe" to convey their absolute dependence upon Jesus and confirms their correct knowledge by stating their surety that He is the Christ, the Son of the living God. Obviously, our understanding of Christ is not complete at conversion, and will increase as we grow in our faith. Even the great apostle Paul, prayed "that I may know Him and the power of His resurrection" (Philippians 3:10). However, knowing that Jesus is God and Savior is the prerequisite knowledge that drives us to believe (trust) on Him.

Now that the differentiation between knowing and believing has been made, you are now equipped to place your response in the self-scout chart. A "yes," recorded for "Know" indicates agreement that Jesus is the sinless, Son of God and Savior of the world. A "yes" for "Believe," indicates that you have placed your trust solely in Christ for salvation.

Beliefs	Demons	Christians	Me?
1. Believe Jesus is the Son of God.	Know: Yes Believe: No	Know: Yes Believe: Yes	Know: Believe:

III. *Belief in the Gospel*

> As we were going to the place of prayer, we were met by a slave girl who had a spirit of divination and brought her owners much gain by fortune-telling.
>
> She followed Paul and us, crying out, "These men are servants of the Most High God, who proclaim to you the way of salvation."
>
> And this she kept doing for many days. Paul, having become greatly annoyed, turned and said to the spirit, "I command you in the name of Jesus Christ to come out of her." And it came out that very hour. (Acts 16:16–18)

Before beginning our discussion on this passage from the book of Acts it is extremely important to first recognize the emphasis Christ placed on believing the gospel message. Mark records that the charge to believe in the gospel was Christ's singular focus as He began His ministry, and the last words Jesus spoke before His ascension included the sobering warning against unbelief in the gospel. Carefully read the following two passages and allow them to arrest your attention on this third and final belief necessary for salvation. Remember, these are the words of Christ Himself!

> Now after that John was put in prison, Jesus came into Galilee, preaching the gospel of the kingdom of God, And saying, The time is fulfilled, and the kingdom of God is at hand: repent ye, and believe the gospel. (Mark 1: 14-15 KJV)
>
> And he said unto them, Go ye into all the world, and preach the gospel to every creature. He that believeth and is baptized shall be saved; but he that believeth not shall be damned. (Mark 16: 15-16 KJV)

Returning to Acts 16:16-18, Luke shares a fascinating account from Paul's second missionary journey. While in Philippi, Paul and Silas were on their way to the local place of prayer and were met by a young girl possessed by a demon. The girl had followed Paul and Silas for many days. As all the people gathered to hear Paul proclaim the Gospel, the girl would periodically interrupt with loud affirmations to the truth of Paul's message and even vouched for his and Silas's character. However, why would a demon want to join with Paul, and show solidarity to his message? Matthew Henry offers his opinion.

> As designed by the evil spirit, that subtle serpent, to the dishonor of the gospel; some think she designed hereby to gain credit to herself and her prophecies, and so to increase her master's profit by pretending to be in the interest of the apostles, who, she thought, had a growing reputation, or to curry favor with Paul, that he might not separate her and her familiar. Others think that Satan, who can transform himself into an angel of light, and can say anything to serve a turn, designed hereby to disgrace the apostles; as if these divines were of the same fraternity with their diviners, because they were witnessed to by them, and then the people might as well adhere to those they had been used to. Those that were most likely to receive the apostles' doctrine were such as were prejudiced against these spirits of divination, and therefore would, by this testimony, be prejudiced against the gospel; and, as for those who regarded these diviners, the devil thought himself sure of them.[71]

---

[71] Matthew Henry, *A Commentary on the Whole Bible* (Peabody; Hendrickson Publishers, 2000), 2136.

Whether the demon's strategy was one of self-preservation or subversion of Paul's message is unknown. What is clear however, is the demon's agreement to the truth of Paul's teaching regarding the "way of salvation," which Paul referred to elsewhere as the Gospel of Jesus Christ (1 Corinthians 9:12).

The word gospel appears over ninety times in the New Testament. It is derived from the Greek word, "euangelion" which actually means "good news." Euangelion is used in the Old Testament as well and was commonly associated with the report of victory in battle. Isaiah 52:7 is a well-known example of its use in this regard, "How beautiful upon the mountains are the feet of him who brings good news."

The announcement of victory is the same theme the word gospel carries with it in the New Testament as well. It is the victory of Jesus Christ over sin, death, and the devil. He accomplished this victory by living a perfect life of obedience and dying an atoning death on the cross. He verified His victory by rising again, sitting down at the Right Hand of Power, and pouring out His Spirit upon the church. This is the magnificent Gospel of Jesus Christ.

Sadly, many today do not understand the significance of the Gospel and therefore reject it. To believe the Gospel as the greatest news ever announced in history, we must understand how our past as human beings not only defines our present reality, but also predicts our future abode.

Understanding our past

The fall of Adam and Eve in the Garden is considered by many, even professing Christians, as little more than creative storytelling. However, it was precisely because of this rebellion that sin and death became the only reality we know. Ironically, it was immediately following the sin of Adam and Eve that the Gospel was first proclaimed to Satan, himself. This initial declaration of victory by God to Satan is often called the protoevangelium and is listed below:

> And I will put enmity between you and the
> woman, and between your offspring and hers; he
> will crush your head, and you will strike his heel.
> (Genesis 3:15)

It took millennia after this declaration was made to the serpent for the Gospel of Christ and His kingdom to be fulfilled. Only God knows the reasons for such a long delay, but proving to us our own depravity, the horrific consequences of sin, and the holiness of God are perhaps at least three reasons.

For much of this time, God was dealing exclusively with the nation of Israel. Their entire history of rebellion and God's long-suffering mercy was a case study that Israel, the representative for the nations, was incapable of keeping the Law and saving themselves, as Paul explains to the Roman church.

> Now we know that whatever the law says
> it speaks to those who are under the law, so that
> every mouth may be stopped, and the whole
> world may be held accountable to God.
> For by works of the law no human being
> will be justified in his sight, since through the
> law comes knowledge of sin. (Romans 3:19–20)

Understanding our present

The inability to earn our way to heaven is our present reality. As a consequence of our past (the fall), we are spiritually dead, totally corrupt and enemies of God. Therefore, our inconsistent and imperfect deeds of obedience are filthy rags in the sight of God, especially when done with the intent of earning salvation (Isaiah 64:6).

This understanding of man's inability to save himself is unique to Christianity. Every other major religion puts forth their own merit system of good works where salvation must be earned by the individual. However, a recent poll conducted in 2020 reveals that an alarming number of American Christians have also embraced a "works-based" theology.

> Most surprising in the latest findings from the American Worldview Inventory 2020 is that a majority of people who describe themselves as Christian (52 percent) accept a "works-oriented" means to God's acceptance. More shocking, huge proportions of people associated with churches whose official doctrine says eternal salvation comes only from embracing Jesus Christ as savior believe that a person can qualify for Heaven by being or doing good. That includes close to half of all adults associated with Pentecostal (46 percent), mainline Protestant (44 percent), and evangelical (41 percent) churches. A much larger share of Catholics (70 percent) embrace that point of view.[72]

These poll results reveal just how far the basic understanding of biblical truth regarding the Gospel has deteriorated. Though the Bible clearly teaches that our obedience is expected and important, it is an evidence of saving faith and not the means of attaining or maintaining salvation. Below are a few verses that clearly teach our salvation is not dependent in any way on our own efforts but rather on belief.

> And by him all that believe are justified from all things, from which ye could not be justified by the law of Moses. (Acts 13:39)

---

[72] Perceptions of Sin and Salvation, Release no. 8, Cultural Research Center at Arizona Christian University, August. 4, 2020.

> Therefore by the deeds of the law there shall no flesh be justified in his sight: for by the law [is] the knowledge of sin. (Romans 3:20)

> Knowing that a man is not justified by the works of the law, but by the faith of Jesus Christ, even we have believed in Jesus Christ, that we might be justified by the faith of Christ, and not by the works of the law: for by the works of the law shall no flesh be justified. (Galatians 2:16 KJV)

> For by grace are ye saved through faith; and that not of yourselves: it is the gift of God: Not of works, lest any man should boast. (Ephesians 2:8, 9 KJV)

As mentioned, a key clue as to whether a person is in bondage to the spiritual stronghold of false-assurance is the belief that they can earn their way into Heaven. This certainly was the case for myself. When my college football coach asked me what I would say to God when I died if He asked me, "Why should I let you in heaven?" I immediately rattled off a list of things I did to earn my spot in heaven.

Though I knew about God, and the deity of Christ my trust for salvation was in my own effort. My understanding was not the "way of salvation," in fact, it was in direct opposition to the Gospel. So before moving on to our next topic, take a moment to honestly consider the same question my coach asked me. If you died today and God asked you why should He let you into heaven, what would you say?

Understanding our future

Our past has not only determined our sinful and helpless present but also sets in stone our horrific fate if belief in God, Christ and the Gospel is cast aside. Of course, I am referring to the reality of hell. Yet just as Adam and Eve, the fall, and the great flood have taken up position as myth in the minds of many professing Christians, so too has hell. Even more so with hell, as that involves an extremely unpleasant reality that deals with them personally. However, returning to the teaching mode of antithetical parallelism, would demons agree with those who scoff at the notion of hell? The following verses prove the demonic realm are convinced of their eventual and miserable fate.

> And when he was come to the other side into the country of the Gergesenes, there met him two possessed with devils, coming out of the tombs, exceeding fierce, so that no man might pass by that way. And, behold, they cried out, saying, What have we to do with thee, Jesus, thou Son of God? art thou come hither to torment us before the time? (Matthew 8:28–29 KJV)

> And cried with a loud voice, and said, What have I to do with thee, Jesus, *thou* Son of the most high God? I adjure thee by God, that thou torment me not. For he said unto him, Come out of the man, *thou* unclean spirit. (Mark 5:7–8 KJV)

> And in the synagogue there was a man, which had a spirit of an unclean devil, and cried out with a loud voice, Saying, Let *us* alone; what have we to do with thee, *thou* Jesus of Nazareth? Art thou come to destroy us? I know thee who thou art; the Holy One of God. (Luke 4:33–34 KJV)

As discussed, many do not come to faith in Christ simply because they don't feel the need. Sure, they have troubles from time to time, but for the most part everything is fine in their lives. They don't need the "crutch" of religion, they can make it just fine on their own. Such people may even acknowledge the existence of God and the deity of Christ, but since they are ignorant of their spiritual condition, they rarely take either seriously. Yet they comfort themselves periodically that their God, is a "God of love," who will never punish anyone. In other words, they don't believe in hell. Based on recent data from the Pew Research Center, this is precisely the case for many Americans of all religious backgrounds.[73]

Religious Tradition	Believe in Hell	Don't Believe in Hell	Unsure	Sample Size
Buddhist	32%	63%	5%	264
Catholic	63%	29%	8%	7,202
Evangelical Protestant	82%	11%	7%	8,593
Hindu	28%	62%	11%	199
Jewish	22%	70%	7%	847
Mainline Protestant	60%	29%	11%	6,083
Mormon	62%	30%	8%	664
Muslim	76%	18%	6%	237

Roughly a third of Catholics, mainline Protestants and Mormons do not believe in Hell, as well as a majority of Jews, Buddhists and Hindus. No hell, no punishment, no need for a Savior or His Gospel. However, as we have seen the demons are not universalists in their theology. Satan and his horde are under no delusion with regards to the reality of hell, but men who are, do so at their great peril as Edwards affirms.

> The devils know God's truth, and there-
> fore they believe his threatenings, and tremble
> in expectation of their accomplishment. And

---

[73] The Pew Research Center, Religious Landscape Study, Washington, DC, 2014.

> wicked men that now doubt his truth, and dare not trust his word, will hereafter, in the most convincing, affecting manner, find his word to be true in all that he has threatened, and will see that he is faithful to his promises in the rewards of his saints.[74]

If you did not mark "yes" for each of the first two beliefs, perhaps it is because no need for a God, let alone a Savior, is felt? Maybe you do believe in a God "of sorts," but that God would never assign anyone to such a horrific fate as hell. The concept of eternal damnation in a real place called hell is absurd, blasphemous even, for many people in our modern society. Even the idea of sin has been whitewashed in the language of addiction, mental illness, genetics or moral relativism. Such ideas come from the spirit of this world, not the Spirit of God. If God's wrath upon sin is not real, then Christ's atoning death was the most cruel and meaningless event to ever occur. However, Jesus did not die in vain, for He knew exactly what was at stake for us.

Theologians rightfully observe that Jesus spoke more on hell than he did on heaven. In fact, no individual in the Scriptures taught more on hell than Jesus did. The following is just one occasion that where Christ conveyed the reality of hell in very fascinating way to his disciples. The context of this account is found in Luke 10.

Jesus had just appointed and empowered seventy-two of His disciples and sent them ahead of Him to various towns he was to visit. He instructed them to preach on the nearness of the kingdom of God. Upon return, they conveyed their jubilation and astonishment that even the demons obeyed them when they gave command in Christ's name.

In response to their excitement on the success of their mission, Jesus affirmed, "I saw Satan fall like lightning from the sky" (Luke 10:18). In other words, Jesus was saying, "I was there when the great

---

[74] Jonathan Edwards, *Tabletalk* (Orlando; Ligonier Ministries, February 1, 2005) Christian Classics.

rebellion happened, and I know what awaits Satan and the demons that followed him."

So, Jesus tells them, "Rejoice that your names are written in heaven" and that your fate will not be as theirs. If one says that hell is not real, then he is saying that Jesus is wrong, or, much worse, that Christ is lying. Both assertions are impossible; and seriously grave assertions for one to make.

Final thoughts

To begin, it is noteworthy that on the night of his betrayal, Jesus affirmed the three critical beliefs necessary for salvation to His apostles, namely, the belief in God, Himself, and the Gospel. This familiar and cherished passage is listed below:

> Let not your heart be troubled: ye believe in God, believe also in me. In my Father's house are many mansions: if it were not so, I would have told you. I go to prepare a place for you. And if I go and prepare a place for you, I will come again, and receive you unto myself; that where I am, there ye may be also. And whither I go ye know, and the way ye know. Thomas saith unto him, Lord, we know not whither thou goest; and how can we know the way? Jesus saith unto him, I am the way, the truth, and the life: no man cometh unto the Father, but by me. (John 14:1–6 KJV)

I will not take the time to set this passage in proper context other than to recognize the extreme fear, sorrow, and disillusion that filled the hearts of the apostles. Christ had just confirmed again that His death was imminent, and again, the apostles started to argue about which one of them would be the greatest!

Even though Jesus had spoken of His death more frequently to this point, the apostles still could not face the reality of it. However, after Christ washed their feet and affirmed that one of them was a devil and would betray Him, that they would all desert Him, and that Peter would deny Him, the gravity of His words finally hit home.

So knowing their fearful hearts, Jesus set aside His own troubled spirit and sought to strengthen the faith of His friends. In the opening verse, Jesus acknowledges His confidence that the apostles had a saving belief in God and commands them to have that same belief and trust in Himself. In the remaining verses, Christ explains that although there are many "mansions" in heaven there is only one way to get there.

It is only the atoning work of Christ on the cross that prepares the way for salvation, for them, and for all mankind. Indeed, no one comes to the Father but by the Son. This is the Gospel message, and it must be believed. To believe, otherwise, proves you remain a thief and a robber (John 10:1) and are still clothed in your own self-righteous wedding garment (Matthew 22:11–13).

Thus, there are two main components that characterize genuine belief. First, a Christian understands his own sinfulness and acknowledges the just penalty for it. That said, remember that faith and assurance exist in degrees and continues to grow with the increasing comprehension of our own fallen nature, and its ramifications if not for the forgiveness of Christ. This is a big part of why our love for and trust in the LORD grows as we mature. The second component that characterizes genuine belief is the understanding that our own good works can never merit salvation. A Christian therefore trusts in Christ's righteousness on his behalf. Again, this is the Gospel, the way of salvation, and the only work necessary is belief.

However, we cannot conjure up this saving belief on our own. Genuine faith (Ephesians 2:8–9; Philippians 1:29) and repentance (Acts 11:18; 2 Timothy 2:25), the requirements for destroying the spiritual stronghold of false-assurance, is a gift granted to us via the quickening of the Spirit of God. Yet God will never force you to place your trust in Him against your will. Consequently, we are presented with a dilemma; we must place our trust in Christ for salvation, but our fallen nature prevents us from doing so. Spurgeon explains how the Holy Spirit solves our conundrum; "Man is not saved against his will, but he is made willing by the Holy Ghost. A mighty grace which he does not wish to resist enters into the man, disarms him, makes a new creature of him, and he is saved."

Indeed, Jesus said all things were possible with God; even the quickening of spiritually dead men and drawing them to Christ for salvation (Matthew 19:26; John 6:44). Therefore, I strongly urge you to ask God for the gift of repentance unto faith. He will most certainly grant your request (John 6:37).

Finally, our exercise in antithetical parallelism proved that the theology of demons is impeccable. They are fully aware and understand the truth of every doctrine and precept of Scripture. Yet this knowledge, will only serve as testimony against them on the day of Judgement. They rejected God eons ago and remain in a permanent and eternal state of hatred and defiance, towards Him. The demons, along with every man who says, "I will not have Christ rule over me" (Luke 19:14), will spend eternity together in the most dreadful of places. However, believers in God, Christ and the Gospel will dwell in mansions of glory for eternity.

As my coach warned me after fully explaining the Gospel to me, I will do so for you. The Bible says, "Today is the day of salvation" (2 Corinthians 6:2) and you may not get another opportunity. Do not let fear, pride or anything prevent you from belief. That said, your completion of the Mindful question at the end of this chapter will be the most important assignment of your life, do not neglect it.

Mindful question

Before you place your final answers in the self-scout chart below, please read Jesus' descriptions of the reality of Hell before deciding whether or not to take your stand alongside the vilest of creatures and suffer the same fate.

1. The Son of Man will send his angels, and they will gather out of his kingdom all causes of sin and all law-breakers, and throw them into the fiery furnace. In that place

there will be weeping and gnashing of teeth. (Matthew 13:41–42)

2. Then he will say to those on his left, "Depart from me, you cursed, into the eternal fire prepared for the devil and his angels." (Matthew 25:41)

Beliefs	Demons	Christians	Me?
Belief in God.	Know: Yes Believe: No	Know: Yes Believe: Yes	Know: Believe:
Belief in Jesus, the Son of God.	Know: Yes Believe: No	Know: Yes Believe: Yes	Know: Believe:
Belief in the Gospel	Know: Yes Believe: No *It's too late for demons to accept Christ as Lord.	Know: Yes Believe: Yes *Genuine Christians believe and place their trust solely on the finished work of Christ for salvation.	Know: Believe: *It's not too late for you!

11

FINAL WALK-THROUGH:
LAST REVIEW

The horse is made ready for the day of battle,
but the victory belongs to the Lord.
                                            —King Solomon

I mentioned that football coaches begin implementation of the key objectives of the game plan, with a very controlled introduction held at the beginning of the week typically called the "Monday Walk-through." The next few days of practice those objectives are implemented continuously at full speed and contact to test their validity, and to prepare the team to execute them on game day. However, the last practice before the game, the key objectives are reviewed one final time, at a much slower pace to avoid any injury and to allow the players to recover physically from a tough week of practice.

Though not physically demanding, this final practice is mentally intense, and is the last opportunity for players to make all of the offensive and defensive checks on their own. This last practice, called the "final walkthrough," instills confidence in the players and coaches that the game plan objectives were implemented properly, and the team is ready to compete.

Consider this last chapter our final walkthrough. We will review the key concepts in our game plan to overcome the five obstacles to the assurance of salvation, make sure you understand them, and are ready to compete!

With this goal in mind, you'll recall that I closed chapter 1 by sharing the Japanese legend of the crane wife to illustrate the great impact a lack of assurance can have on a believer. Similarly, in this final chapter, my goal is to crystalize in your mind all the topics we discussed in our game plan for overcoming the spiritual stronghold of assurance-doubt. However, this time, I will call upon Greek mythology and tell the story of Hercules and his battle with the Nemean lion and the Lernaean Hydra.

For those unfamiliar with the lore of Hercules, it's best to provide some background information on this legendary hero. According to Greek mythology, Hercules was the son of the supreme god Zeus, but his mother was Alcmene, granddaughter of the hero Perseus. Thus, Hercules had an earthly and heavenly nature. The story of Hercules began when he was unjustly sentenced to perform twelve challenges or labors to atone for crimes that were not entirely his fault.

For his first challenge, Hercules had to defeat the Nemean lion, a vicious beast that terrorized the area of Nemea for years. Hercules was a skilled hunter and had tracked and killed many ferocious animals, but this predator was unlike any he had faced before. After many days searching for the lion, Hercules finally saw it emerge from its den. The lion was enormous and charged Hercules with alarming speed. Raising his bow, Hercules let several arrows fly in succession. Each one hit its target but did not penetrate the thick hide of the beast. The lion was enraged and was now almost upon Hercules. Hercules raised his war club and brought it down with tremendous force upon the lion's skull. Such a blow would have instantly killed any other animal, but it only stunned the huge cat. Nevertheless, the lion retreated to its den. Hercules pursued the lion and barricaded the exit of the den with large rocks. Hercules then went bravely down into the lion's den, knowing full well that his weapons would be of no use in this battle. To kill this beast, he would have to do so with his bare hands. The two combatants fought for what seemed like hours in the dank, dark cave until Hercules was finally able to choke the lion to death with the great strength of his arms.

After his victory, the goddess Athena told Hercules to skin the scourge of Nemea with one of its own claws and to use its hide as armor in his future challenges. In fact, almost all ancient depictions of Hercules show him clad not in traditional armor but with the skin of the Nemean lion draped over his shoulders and the animal's massive head pulled up over his own like a helmet. This armor would greatly aid and protect Hercules in his much more difficult clash with the Lernaean Hydra.

For his second labor, Hercules had to travel to the city of Lerna, which was located on the shore of a huge ancient lake. Under its murky waters lay the entrance to the underworld, which was guarded by the dreaded Lernaean Hydra. The Hydra was a fearsome snake-like creature with nine heads. It was created specifically by the wicked goddess Hera to not only guard the underworld, but as she was the avowed enemy of Hercules, she also bred it specifically to kill him. Nonetheless, it was Hercules's responsibility to enter the swampy lair of the monster and subdue it.

In his battle with the Hydra, every time Hercules cut off one of its heads, two more would grow back in its place. Growing frustrated with his inability to slay the monster, Hercules tried a different approach. To divert and confuse the beast, he set its lair on fire. However, Hera countered by sending Korkinos, a huge and ferocious crab, to distract Hercules from killing her prized serpent. Hercules now had two monsters to battle!

Recognizing his inability to defeat both monsters, Hercules sought the aid of Iolaus, his nephew, to help him kill the giant crab. After defeating Korkinos, the duo then turned their full attention to the Hydra. Hercules instructed his nephew to burn the neck of each head that Hercules severed, thereby preventing it from growing back. However, to finally kill the beast, Hercules must cut off its one immortal head. To do that, Hercules would need the golden sword of Athena. Unlike Hera, Athena was a just goddess who loved and protected Hercules and so was pleased to provide him with her golden sword. Thus, with the aid of his nephew, the goddess Athena, and the golden sword, Hercules finally severed the immortal head and killed the Lernaean Hydra. However, the immortal head still clung to life, so Hercules buried it under a huge stone to keep it from regaining its former power.

Now that I finished telling this story, I will explain its interpretation in the context of the critical topics we have discussed in our game plan. First, we will examine the person of Hercules himself. Like us, Hercules had both an earthly and a heavenly nature. Therefore, the very dichotomy we struggle against was the same battle Hercules had to face. In fact, historians and experts in mythology recognize the real meaning of the twelve labors of Hercules as man's continuing battle over his own fallen nature. Indeed, the two main premises of our game plan to overcome the obstacles to assurance lie in our ability to master the negative synergy of our own fallen thoughts, emotions, and actions.

To that end, just as Hercules was tasked with entering the den of the Nemean lion and the lair of the Hydra to slay them, we too are commanded to enter the spiritual stronghold of assurance-doubt and destroy it (2 Peter 1:10–11). However, we discussed that overcoming spiritual strongholds requires spiritual armor. As mentioned, the allegorical interpretation of the story of Hercules is man's ongoing quest to master the sin that would master him. However, we dare not attempt such a task in our own strength. Thus, we see another parallel with Hercules. While Hercules was protected by the pelt of the Nemean lion, our armor is provided by the greater lion of Judah (Ephesians 6:10–18)! Nevertheless, to be effective, we must put our spiritual armor on by faith and get in the battle for our assurance and use it! Just as God commanded Cain to master the *crouching lion* of sin within him (Genesis 4:6–7 KJV), our charge as Christians is the same (2 Peter 1:5–11). This determined effort to obey Christ is required to overcome the first obstacle to assurance we discussed— *uncommitted in walk*.

Continuing with our parallels, many historians see Hercules's first labor with the Nemean lion as an illustration of man's continuing battle with his own destructive emotions. You'll recall that the weapons of Hercules could not make quick work of the fierce beast. In fact, they were entirely ineffective against the Nemean lion. Hercules had to kill his foe the hard way—with his bare hands, so too in our struggles with our own destructive emotions. There is no room for shortcuts, excuse-making, blame-shifting, or disingenuous repentance. Let the imagery of Hercules's great struggle against the Nemean lion help you contemplate the issues we discussed regarding the second obstacle to assurance—*unrestored in emotions*.

Whereas negative emotions were personified in the Nemean lion, the battle with the Lernaean Hydra is often understood as man's struggle to master the erroneous thoughts and uncertainties present within his own mind. To that end, I will now examine this second and arguably most difficult labor of Hercules. Again, I will do so, considering the topics we discussed in overcoming the obstacles of being *unbiblical in foundation* and *undisciplined in mind*.

To begin, remember that in chapter 9 we emphasized that for assurance to be achieved, we must be able to comprehend and apprehend the promises and evidence of salvation. Regarding apprehension, we discussed the great impact negative core beliefs, cognitive distortions, and intrusive thoughts have on our ability to personally claim the guarantees of eternal security.

Therefore, think of the immortal head of the Hydra as your own negative core beliefs. The immortal head, even when severed, still had a spark of life within it, requiring Hercules to bury it beneath a huge stone. This is a very powerful illustration affirming the difficulty we encounter when we do the arduous work of reframing our negative core beliefs with the Word of God. Remember, negative core beliefs die hard and will do everything they can to cling to life. However, it is the part of you that must be buried beneath the great stone of the Scriptures.

Next, all the lesser heads of the serpent can be understood as representing our unique cognitive distortions. As we noted in chapter 9, cognitive distortions emanate ultimately from negative core beliefs and seek to defend and justify them. Therefore, such thoughts normally must be dispatched with first before negative core beliefs can be effectively addressed. So our hero and his nephew had to first remove these subordinate heads before they could gain access to the immortal head.

Interestingly, you will recall that the beast Korkinos was sent by Hera to distract Hercules from cutting off the immortal head of the Hydra. Thus, Korkinos represents the distracting intrusive thoughts that obsessive thinkers create in their minds to prevent them from facing highly stressful situations. Like cognitive distortions, the ultimate purpose of intrusive thoughts is to protect the "immortal head" of our negative core beliefs from being exposed and defeated.

Therefore, within our own minds reside both the Hydra and Korkinos. However, in this analogy, we are also Hercules. We must do battle with both beasts if we are to apprehend the promises and evidence of our salvation! Remember, to overcome the obstacle of being *undisciplined in mind,* we must become mature and disciplined in our thinking. Therefore, I highly recommend to commit the following verses to memory:

> When I was a child, I spoke like a child, I thought like a child, I reasoned like a child. When I became a man, I gave up childish ways. (1 Corinthians 13:11)

> Brothers, do not be children in your thinking. Be infants in evil, but in your thinking be mature. (1 Corinthians 14:20)

> Wherefore gird up the loins of your mind, be sober, and hope to the end for the grace that is to be brought unto you at the revelation of Jesus Christ. (1 Peter 1:13 KJV)

To achieve assurance, we must also comprehend that our salvation is an eternal promise of God and that there is nothing that can prevent a promise of God from being fulfilled. However, we stated several times that although Satan knows he cannot prevent our salvation, he nonetheless can cause us to doubt it. Thus, Hera represents the wicked Satanic harassment we can expect when we engage the spiritual stronghold of assurance-doubt. Importantly, the aid of

Iolaus conveys our need to be humble enough to seek assistance in our struggle to make our calling and election sure.

Finally, I will conclude the analogy with the goddess Athena and the golden sword. Athena represents the Holy Spirit. Just as the benevolent goddess was always on the ready to help Hercules, the Holy Spirit empowers, illuminates, sanctifies, and seals every believer. The golden sword of Athena is the Word of God. The spirit of God illuminates our minds with the promises of salvation and builds into our lives the virtuous evidence of our salvation. Both are done via the sanctifying power Word of God (John 17:17). It is the power of the Holy Spirit that enables us to fully comprehend the promises and evidence of our eternal security put forth in the Scriptures, thereby overcoming the obstacle of being *unbiblical in foundation.*

I hope the imagery of this ancient Greek legend will help you remember the key themes we have discussed in our game plan and the four specific obstacles believers must overcome to attain the assurance of salvation. Therefore, in pursuit of that ultimate prize, let's continue with our final walk-through and review.

Synergy review

I said early on, and will repeat it now, that if you take anything away from this book let it be a deep appreciation of the reality and power of synergy! The synergistic relationship between our thoughts, emotions, and actions is a key concept to understand whether one struggles with the assurance of salvation or not. As we have seen, the Bible has myriad allusions to such synergy. In addition, we have seen that this underlying relationship is the foundation for most psychotherapy modalities. Indeed, the two major premises of our game plan are centered on the synergy of thought, emotions, and actions:

1. The synergism (negative) of our thoughts, emotions, and actions is a key factor in the formation of spiritual strongholds and increases the difficulty for tearing them down.
2. The cycle of synergy starts regardless of the initial impetus. Whether our thoughts, emotions, or actions kick start the

cycle, the other two will be impacted, and the end result will be the same—the formation/strengthening of a spiritual stronghold.

In chapter 18 and section 3 of the WCF, "Of Assurance of Grace and Salvation," the divines acknowledged that a *"true believer may wait long and conflict with many difficulties before he be a partaker of it"* [assurance]. Thus, it is the negative synergy that exists within our thoughts, emotions, and actions which is the mechanism responsible for the often delayed and difficult attainment of assurance.

Spiritual strongholds and spiritual armor review

As confirmed in the two key premises of our game plan, synergy is foundational to the development and defense of spiritual strongholds such as assurance-doubt and false-assurance. Remember as well, that both strongholds we discussed are supremely powerful delusions that Satan has been using for millennia.

His tactics to defend these wicked footholds are intimidation (the lion's den) on one extreme, and subterfuge (the enchanted ground) on the other. Both are very effective; therefore, you must be aware when each scheme is being deployed. However, being successful against those schemes, and tearing down spiritual strongholds requires spiritual weapons; and the empowerment of the Holy Spirit.

Ultimately, it is only through the power of God that strongholds can be torn down. However, since the "old man" is complicit in the formation and defense of the stronghold of assurance-doubt, the "new man" must also play a role in tearing it down. To accomplish this daunting task, God has granted us His spiritual armor, and the aide of His Spirit. The spiritual stronghold of assurance-doubt cannot remain standing when the Spirit of the Living God has empowered a fully armed and determined Christian!

Below is a reminder of your spiritual armor and its specificity to overcome each of the obstacles of assurance-doubt, as well as the steps that are necessary to tear down the two strongholds of assurance-doubt and false-assurance.

Thoughts *Unbiblical in Foundation* *Undisciplined in Mind*	Emotions *Unrestored* *in Emotions*	Actions *Uncommitted in Walk*
Belt of truth	Breastplate of righteousness	Shoes of the gospel of peace
Helmet of salvation	Shield of faith	Sword of the Spirit

Five Obstacles to the Assurance of Salvation	Steps for Destroying the Spiritual Stronghold of Assurance-Doubt	Steps for Destroying the Spiritual Stronghold of False-Assurance
• Uncommitted in Walk	Refuse to live in disobedience.	
• Unrestored in Emotions	Reject fear and other negative emotions.	
• Unbiblical in Foundation • Undisciplined in Mind	Replace all lies/errors with the Truth of God.	
• Unsaved in Reality		Repent and believe.

Spiritual stronghold of assurance-doubt review

To begin our review of the spiritual stronghold of assurance-doubt, I will remind you of the first two types of people described by Sproul:

1. Those who are saved and know they are.
2. Those who are saved but don't think they are.

The first four objectives (obstacles) we discussed are most relevant for Sproul's second category of people. We have seen through an extensive study of the Word of God that these genuine believers have lost their assurance because of the following:

1. Disobedience and/or negligence (*uncommitted in walk*).
   - Key hurdles to overcome: legalism, license, and lethargy.
2. Unresolved emotional issues (*unrestored in emotions*).
   - Key hurdles to overcome: fear's ability to cause doubt, distraction, and devolution.
3. Misunderstanding of Scripture (*unbiblical in foundation*).
   - Key hurdles to overcome: rejection of the eternal promises and evidences of salvation.
4. Innate thinking errors (*undisciplined in mind*).
   - Key hurdles to overcome: negative core beliefs, cognitive distortions, and intrusive thoughts.

Because of the synergy between our thoughts, emotions, and actions it is highly likely that Christians who struggle with assurance must overcome each of these four obstacles to destroy the spiritual stronghold of assurance-doubt.

For those Christians who have never doubted their salvation (Sproul's first category), understanding these four obstacles will help them counsel those who do, as well as guard their own continued assurance. To that end I pray that every pastor and/or counselor would understand and communicate the concepts presented in this book to those in their circle of influence who need it most!

Evaluating your progress

There is a saying in football, "the eye in the sky doesn't lie." This refers to how the game film records each and every play—the good and the bad! Coaches painstakingly assess their players' execution of the key objectives during post-game film sessions. Though these evaluative meetings can get heated, the goal is always to elevate the individual's and team's progress.

Indeed, all good game plans have tools to evaluate the success of the implementation of the key objectives. To that end, the final TEA graph displaying all the requirements for genuine believers to attain and maintain their assurance will be a very helpful tool.

The completed TEA graph below will not only serve as a reminder of the synergy that exists between our thoughts, emotions and actions, but will also be highly beneficial as an aid to pinpoint any lingering and/or future struggles with assurance. Remember the dangers of getting lost in the "enchanted ground?" Think of this final TEA graph as your compass to get you back on course.

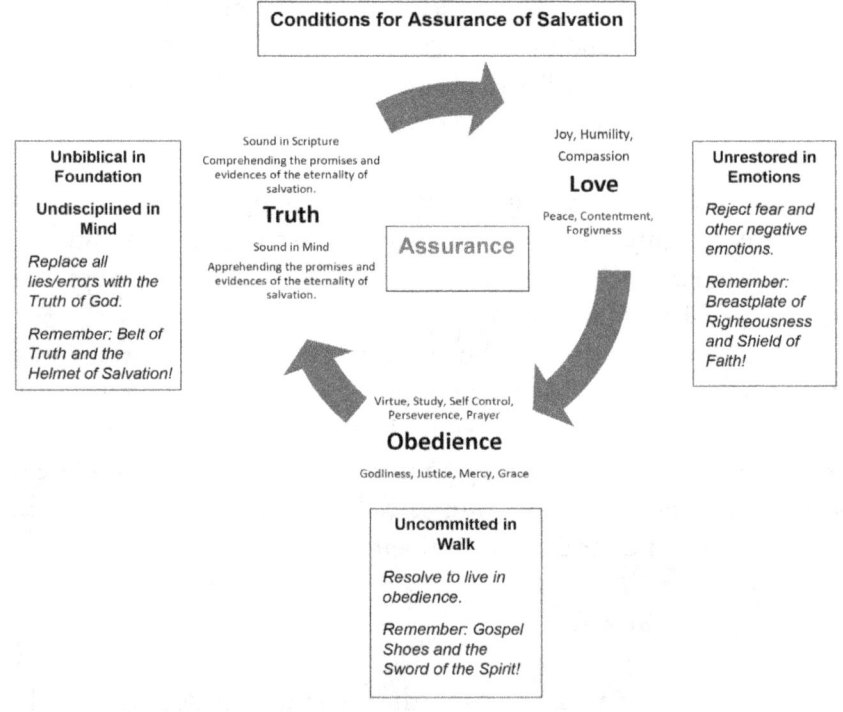

Using the TEA graph

I often return to this completed TEA graph, and meditatively consider how I am measuring up to the necessary requirements of truth, love, and obedience along with the key features of each. The visual nature of the final TEA graph provides similar benefits as does a football film coaching session, and keeps me focused on the key objectives necessary for assurance. I mentioned that coaches can get very intense pointing out areas that need to be improved during film sessions. However, the best coaches get even more animated with the praise they heap upon their players for things done well. You need to have that same level of intensity as you assess your own progress with the completed TEA graph. Acknowledge and confess your shortcomings, but don't forget to encourage yourself and praise God for you progress!

I normally begin my self-examination with the general category of, "Actions." I begin the process by asking myself a few pointed questions to soberly assess how I am measuring up with each key attribute of "Obedience." During this self-scout, I call to mind the spiritual armor of God and remind myself of the requirements for tearing down spiritual strongholds. Meditating on the imagery and function of each piece of armor and visualizing yourself wearing them is very helpful. What follows, then, is some practical advice on how to conduct your own self-scout using the completed TEA graph.

Sometimes I begin the process as Peter did, with virtue and knowledge. I ask myself if there are any obvious sins in my life? Have I been diligent in my study of the Word, and what has the Holy Spirit been teaching me? How consistent has my prayer time been? By the way, seeing the parallels of praying in the Spirit with the imagery of the Roman march has greatly helped the consistency of my prayers.

I occasionally enjoy a cigar, a glass of wine, or a good craft beer; therefore, I ask myself if I am applying Paul's three principles of self-control to any adiaphorous behaviors I engage in? Finally, but most importantly, is my behavior towards others consistent with the commands of God (my North Star verses)?

To experience victory in these areas and others that fall into this category requires one to take action. Therefore, meditating on the imagery associated with the Gospel Shoes and the Sword of the Spirit discussed in chapter 5 is a powerful way to work through your self-scout.

After considering my actions, I normally move on to my thoughts. Is my mind governed by the truth of God? It is so easy for the philosophies and cares of this world to creep into our thoughts. We must be determined to frame all of our thinking in a biblical reality. When vain ideas capture your attention gird up the loins of your mind (1 Peter 1:13), tighten up the Belt of Truth and squeeze them out! Remember, when opposing philosophies clash, someone's right and someone is wrong; someone's lying, and someone is telling the truth. Let God be true and every man a liar (Rom. 3:4a)!

Though I have made much progress in combating the effects of my particular negative core beliefs, cognitive distortions, and obsessive compulsiveness it still requires a conscious and consistent disciplining of my mind, especially during periods of stress. That said, I prioritize a return to this completed TEA graph when I am confronted with significance challenges. It is especially important to have your Helmet of Salvation on during calamitous times, to focus your mind on each aspect of your salvation.

Finally, I move on to my emotions. Is love or fear ruling my spirit? Remember, all emotions spring from those two parents. Our emotions are our thermostat; therefore, I try to immediately trace any negative emotions I am feeling back to its source.

Am I experiencing any bitterness, envy, unforgiveness, etc.? Journaling, conversing with another individual or even out loud with yourself is very helpful when you can't pinpoint or articulate fully the emotions you're feeling. Once identified, visualize that negative emotion as a "flaming arrow" stuck to your Breastplate of Righteousness and rip it out! Also don't forget to resoak your Shield of Faith with the Word to guard against other flaming arrows of negative emotions.

The completed TEA graph is a very valuable "self-scout" tool whether one struggles with assurance or not. It is an extremely important tool for those with OCD, as it provides a clear visual to objectively assess whether assurance-doubts are coming from one of the obstacles or simply due to their condition.

I have just explained how I incorporate the completed TEA graph, but you must use it in a manner that works best for yourself.

That said, remember the importance of "Goldwyn's gap"; just knowing this final TEA graph is helpful means nothing if you don't use it!

Spiritual stronghold of false-assurance review

Once again, we will start our review of the spiritual stronghold of false-assurance with a reminder of Sproul's last two categories of people:

3. Those who are unsaved and know they aren't.
4. Those who are unsaved but think they are.

The fifth and final obstacle we discussed, *unsaved in reality*, is mainly specific for the fourth category of people described by Sproul, those not yet in a state of grace but think they are. These individuals are prisoners of this formidable spiritual stronghold. In many respects, Sproul's third category of people, those who are unsaved and know it, are much closer to the kingdom of God than those in the fourth!

Nevertheless, we all at one point were unsaved, and must overcome the obstacle of *unsaved in reality* for salvation, let alone assurance, to be achieved. To overcome this obstacle, the only work that needs to be done on our part is to repent and believe. Only the Holy Spirit of God can make repentance from all false beliefs possible and move us to genuine belief in Christ (John 6:44). Below is a reminder of the three critical beliefs that comprise the total work of belief required by God for salvation.

1. Belief in God (Psalms 14:1; Hebrews 11:6)
2. Belief in Christ (John 6:29; Acts 4:12)
3. Belief in the Gospel (Mark 1:15; Mark 16:15-16)

Final thoughts

In conclusion, we have covered much ground in this book, and I applaud you for working your way through each chapter! We have seen that struggles with assurance have been prevalent in the lives of both Old Testament and New Testament saints and countless others since.

This work has also shown from a scriptural and scientific perspective, how the synergistic relationship between our thoughts, emotions, and actions are responsible for struggles with assurance and explains why such struggles can be difficult to endure and overcome. Make no mistake, overcoming the obstacles to assurance can be hard work at times, and our efforts will be undermined by the old man, the world, and the devil. Despite the difficulty, it is our cross to take up until our assurance has been won.

Though we are commanded to work out our own salvation (Philippians 2:12–13) and to make our own calling and election sure (2 Peter 1:10) we cannot do this in our own strength. In fact, our own fallen nature, the demonic realm, and the world we live in make it impossible. The Holy Spirit must enable us to live a godly life, to enlighten us in the Word, and to heal us mentally and emotionally.

With that in mind, please understand that the various graphs and tables I have used throughout this book are merely to help visualize and understand the obstacles to assurance. They are certainly not meant to dismiss or minimize the necessity of the Holy Spirit's power to overcome them.

We need the power of God to overcome all the obstacles involving our thoughts, emotions, and actions for assurance to be achieved. Paul makes abundantly clear in his prayer for the Ephesian church, that the power of God is prerequisite for us to be *rooted and grounded in love* (emotions), to comprehend and *know the love of Christ* (thoughts), and to be *filled with all the fullness of God* (actions). As Solomon said, "The horse is made ready for the day of battle but the victory belongs with the LORD."

This utter dependence on the power of God is especially true for my fellow OCD brothers and sisters, who in my humble opinion, are at a much greater risk for developing profound issues with assurance-doubt. In many respects, the challenges of OCD can be considered a separate obstacle to overcome to gain the assurance of salvation. However, those of us with OCD are still accountable to the command to make our calling and election sure. That said, God will supply greater grace to those who struggle in this regard or who have any other "thorn in the flesh"; for His power is made perfect in weakness (2 Corinthians 12:9).

Below is Paul's aforementioned prayer for the Ephesian church in its entirety. This tremendous passage of Scripture will not only serve as my closing remarks of our game plan for assurance but is also my sincere prayer for you as you continue in your battle to overcome the five obstacles to the assurance of salvation.

> For this reason, I bow my knees before the Father, from whom every family in heaven and on earth is named, that according to the riches of his glory he may grant you to be strengthened with power through his Spirit in your inner being, so that Christ may dwell in your hearts through faith—that you, being rooted and grounded in love, may have strength to comprehend with all the saints what is the breadth and length and height and depth, and to know the love of Christ that surpasses knowledge, that you may be filled with all the fullness of God.
>
> Now to him who is able to do far more abundantly than all that we ask or think, according to the power at work within us, to him be glory in the church and in Christ Jesus throughout all generations, forever and ever. Amen. (Ephesians 3:14–21)

BIBLIOGRAPHY

Allen, James. *As a Man Thinketh*. New York: Barnes and Nobel, 2007.

Amen, Daniel. *Change Your Brain, Change Your Life*. New York: Harmony Books, 2015.

Augustin, Aurelius. "De Dono Perseverantiae, A Tratise on the Gift of Perseverence." *Nicene and Post Nicene Fathers*. Washington, DC: Christian Classics Ethereal Library, April 1, 2012.

Barna, George. "Americans Describe Their Views About Life After Death." *The Barna Group*, 2009.

Bassett, Lucinda. *From Panic to Power*. New York: HarperCollins Publishers, 2001.

Beck, Judith. *Cognitive Behavioral Therapy, Basics and Beyond 3rd edition*. New York: The Guilford Press, 2021.

—. *Cognitive Therapy: Basics and Beyond*. New York: The Guilford Press, 1995.

Beeke, Joel. *Knowing and Growing in Assurance of Faith*. Fearn, Ross-Shire: Christian Focus Publications, 2017.

Betts, J. Gordon et al. *Anatomy and Physiology*. Houston: Rice University, 2022.

Bunyan, John. *Grace Abounding to the Chief of Sinners*. London: The Religious Tract Society, 1905.

Burgo, Joseph. "The Difference Between Guilt and Shame." *Psychology Today*, May 30, 2023.

Burns, David. *Feeling Good: The New Mood Therapy*. New York: Avon Books, 1999.

Burrow, Peter. *Core Beliefs*. Milton QLD: Burrow and Associates, 2012.

Butle, Jimmie. r, *90 Percent of Organizations Fail to Execute Their Strategies Successfully: A White Paper to Help You Avoid Being a Statistic.* Mclean, August 24, 2022.

Calvin, John. *Commentaries on the Catholic Epistles.* Princeton: Princeton Theological Seminary Library, 2009.

Center, The Pew Research. *Religious Landscape Study.* Washington, DC: The Pew Research Center, 2014.

Cloud, Henry. *Changes That Heal.* Grand Rapids: Zondervan, 1992.

Cloud, Henry, and John Towsend. *How People Grow.* Grand Rapids: Zondervan, 2001.

Edwards, Jonathan. *The Devils Believe and Shudder.* Orlando: Ligonier Ministries, 2005.

Ferguson, Sinclair. "Salvation, Past, Present and Future." *Tabletalk*, 2004.

Ferguson, Sinclair. "The Reformation and Assurance." *The Banner of Truth*, 2017: 20.

Geisler, Norman. *Four Views on Eternal Security.* Grand Rapids: Zondervan, 2002.

Gregg, Steve. *Revelation Four Views, A Parallel Commentary.* Nashville: Thomas Nelson Publishers, 1997.

Groeschel, Craig. *Winning the War in Your Mind.* Grand Rapids: Zondervan Books, 2021.

Hadhazy, Adam. "Think Twice: How the Gut's "Second Brain" Influences Mood and Well-Being." *Scientific American*, February 12, 2010.

Henry, Matthew. *Commentary on the Whole Bible.* Peabody: Hendrickson Publishers, 2000.

Hodge, A. A. *The Westminster Confession: A Commentary.* Carlisle: The Banner of Truth Trust, 2002.

Horton, Michael; Geisler, Norman; Ashby, Stephen; Harper, Steven; Pinson, Matthew; Gundry, Stanly. *Four Views: On Eternal Security.* Grand Rapids: Zondervan, 2002.

Howson, John S. *The Metaphors of St. Paul.* London: Hodder and Stoughton, 1883.

Keller, Tim. *3 Objections to the Doctrine of Election.* September 21, 2015.

Kluge, Jeffrey. "Pandemic Anxiety Is Fueling OCD Symptoms—Even for People Without the Disorder," *Time*. n.d.

Kopple, Joel D. "The Biblical View of the Kidney." *American Journal of Nephrology*, 1994: 279–281.

Kornfield, Jack. *The Art of Forgiveness, Lovingkindness and Peace.* London: Bantom, 2008.

Letham, Robert. *The Westminster Assembly Reading Its Theology in Historical Context.* Phillipsburg: P&R Publishing Company, 2009.

Luther, Martin. *A Commentary on Saint Paul's Epistle to the Galatians.* London: B. Blake, 2009.

MacArthur, John. *Love: The Key to Obedience.* October 10, 1991.

—. "Proof of Salvation." *Proof of Salvation.* Paris, TN: The Center for Biblical Counseling and Discipleship, May 17, 2022.

—. *Saved without a Doubt: Being Sure of Your Salvation.* Colorado Springs: Cook Communications Ministries, 2006.

—. "What kind of things do and do not prove the genuineness of saving faith?" Grace to You, n.d.

MacLaren, Alexander. "The Power of Diligence (2 Peter 1:5)." *Blue Letter Bible.* February 17, 2022. www.blueletterbible.org (accessed February 17, 2022).

Moreland, J. P. *Love Your God with All Your Mind: The Role of Reason in the Life of the Soul.* Colorado Springs: NavPress, 1997.

Nebraska Medicine, Behavioral Health. "What Are Intrusive Thoughts, and Are They Normal?" June 13, 2023.

Nestadt G., Kamath V., Maher BS, Krasnow J., Nestadt P., Wang Y., Bakker A., Samuels J. "Doubt and the decision-making process in obsessive-compulsive disorder." *Med Hypotheses*, 2016: 96:1–4.

Osborn, Ian. *Can Christianity Cure Obsessive-Compulsive Disorder?* Ada: Baker Publishing Group, 2008.

Piper, John. *How Do We Pray in the Spirit.* Desiring God Foundation, August 2, 2021.

Poll, The Harris. *Americans Belief in God.* Washington, DC: The Harris Poll, 2006.

—. "Americans Belief in God." n.d.

Sayer, Rob, *Strategic Planning and Strategy Execution: Football Does It Better!* Chicago, September 17, 2012.

Schmidt, H. J. "Crusade Decisions: Counting and Accounting for Lost Sheep." *Journal of the American Society for Church Growth*, 1990: 16–40.

Schwartz, Jeffery. *Brain Lock.* New York: Harper Collins, 2016.

Schwartz, Jeffrey. *You are Not Your Brain.* London: Penguin Books, 2012.

Smith, Chuck. *blueletterbible.org.* June 1, 2005. (accessed May 23, 2023).

Sproul, R. C. *The Holiness of God, Chosen by God, Pleasing God.* Peabody: Hendickson Publishers, 1985.

Spurgeon, Charles. "The Charles Spurgeon Sermon Collection." *The Charles Spurgeon Sermon Collection.* n.d. (accessed July 14, 2023).

Strombeck, J. F. *Shall Never Perish: Eternal Security Examined.* Grand Rapids: Kregal Publications, 1991.

Strong, James. n.d.

Vander Schaaf, Sarah. "Lots of Americans have fear of flying. There are ways to overcome the anxiety disorder." *The Washington Post*, October 12, 2019: Health.

Winston, Sally, and Seif Martin. *Overcoming Unwanted Intrusive Thoughts.* Oakland: New Harbinger Publications, 2017.

ABOUT THE AUTHOR

Frank has over thirty years of experience in the pharmaceutical and biotech industry and coaching football at the college and
high school levels. He holds undergraduate and graduate degrees in
biology, as well as a master's degree in theology, from the Reformed
Presbyterian Theological Seminary. Frank is married to his wife,
Coleen, and together they have four children—Jonathan, Samuel,
Abigail, and Elisabeth.

www.ingramcontent.com/pod-product-compliance
Lightning Source LLC
Chambersburg PA
CBHW031808181224
19222CB00026B/376